PERSONAL NAMES STUDIES OF MEDIEVAL EUROPE:

SOCIAL IDENTITY AND FAMILIAL STRUCTURES

PERSONAL NAMES STUDIES OF MEDIEVAL EUROPE:

SOCIAL IDENTITY AND FAMILIAL STRUCTURES

Edited by
George T. Beech, Monique Bourin,
and Pascal Chareille

2002
Studies in Medieval Culture XLIII
Medieval Institute Publications

WESTERN MICHIGAN UNIVERSITY

Kalamazoo, Michigan USA 49008-5432

Library of Congress Cataloging-in-Publication Data

Personal names studies of medieval Europe : social identity and familial
structures / edited by George T. Beech, Monique Bourin, and Pascal
Chareille.
     p. cm. -- (Studies in medieval culture ; 43)
Includes bibliographical references.
  ISBN 1-58044-063-0 (alk. paper) -- ISBN 1-58044-064-9 (pbk. : alk.
paper)
  1. Names, Personal--France. 2. Names, Personal--Spain. 3. Names,
Personal--Italy. 4. Romance languages--Etymology--Names. 5.
Onomastics. 6. Europe, Southern--History. 7. Middle Ages--History. I.
Beech, George. II. Bourin, Monique, 1944– III. Chareille, Pascal. IV.
Series.
  CB351.S83 vol.43
  [CS2693]
  929.4'094--dc21

                           2002004599

ISBN 1-58044-063-0 (casebound)
ISBN 1-58044-064-9 (paperbound)

CONTENTS

FOREWORD

A truism of medieval scholarship is that observing ordinary medieval people making choices and giving meaning to important aspects of their lives is almost impossible for the modern historian. Written sources, produced largely by a clerical elite and concerned primarily with the affairs of the great, leave the vast majority of the population of Europe known to us at best only by their names, recorded in lists of witnesses to legal proceedings, in tax rolls, or in liturgical texts. And yet in the evidence of personal names, we see how not only kings and aristocrats, but townspeople and peasants, made meaningful choices about their offspring, selecting from within the multiple influences of family, tradition, regional custom, and Church instruction. Medieval naming followed complex patterns but never "rules"—decisions about how to designate children involved complicated strategies which, with patience and skill, can be partially recovered and thus provide insights into otherwise impenetrable areas of medieval social values.

The study of anthroponomy is a vast and daunting discipline, requiring both macro-level statistical studies of name pools of regions and social strata, as well as micro-studies of the onomastic patterns of individual families. It is also a study of the *longue durée*: patterns become meaningful only when considered across the slow generational rhythm of human cultural reproduction. For well over a decade, an international team of scholars under the leadership of Monique Bourin has been following these trajectories, elaborating a methodology for the exploitation of onomastic evidence and presenting, in a series of regional studies, their preliminary conclusions. The present volume is the first presentation of the approaches and results of this scholarly team to an English language readership.

As we learn in these essays, names are central to individual and group identity. And yet the study of anthroponomy is not the same as the study of identity: it is rather only one representation of identity. Very gradually, from early medieval single names, Europeans in many regions developed the tradition of a family or surname, or *nomen paternum*, in addition to a first name. However, as these methodologically sophisticated and sensitive studies show, there are no easy answers to questions about the emergence of naming patterns, or patronymics, of the selection of personal names from parents, grandparents, other kin, regional or international saints, or the like. Similarly there are no "rules" that governed how individual families assigned names to their children. Even such fundamental questions as who chose names (father, mother, godparent?)—or whether people were actually called by the names in everyday activities by which they appear in written sources rather than by nicknames forever lost to us—cannot be completely resolved. And yet in spite of these perplexing difficulties, the scholars represented in this volume offer examples of the important results that can come from serious studies of names and naming. At the same time, their studies should be seen as methodological models for conducting this research. One hopes that the presentation of this vast and important field to an English-reading public will challenge future scholars with a tantalizing view of how name studies can open new vistas into the social and cultural worlds of ordinary men and women of the Middle Ages.

PATRICK GEARY

PREFACE

The thirteen articles in this collection were presented as part of a colloquium entitled "Personal Name Studies and the History of the Family" during the 32nd International Congress on Medieval Studies at Western Michigan University, Kalamazoo, in May 1997. A brief sketch of the historical background leading to this colloquium will help to set it in context.

The study of personal names in the Middle Ages has long been a respected but marginal part of medieval scholarship as a whole. Ever since the development of medieval studies as an academic discipline in the nineteenth century, scholars have sought to understand how medieval people named their children: what stocks of names were available to them, what factors and considerations guided them in their choices, how these latter changed over time, etc. Until relatively recently the predominant interest was in the primordial question of the linguistic origins and development of personal names, the elements and words which went into their formation, and this explains why onomastics was largely the domain of linguists and philologists. In the past two decades however, historians—who had previously neglected the subject—have come to take an increasing interest in it. Progressively they have realized that the drastic changes which had taken place in personal naming over the course of time from late Rome to the Renaissance had neither been dated precisely nor adequately understood. In the western Empire during the fourth through the sixth centuries, the sophisticated Roman practice of double/triple naming had been replaced by Germanic single naming practices which then in turn, after four to five centuries of dominance, gave way to the two-element system (personal plus family name) as it has evolved into our own day. And in the process the name stocks themselves—the repertories of different names in use at any given time—were transformed. Whereas we see as our own the leading names of the later Middle Ages, those of the seventh and eighth centuries are almost completely unrecognizable to us. Another obscure subject was that of feminine naming. A strong impulse for deeper inquiry into these subjects has come from the development of family history in medieval studies in the past two decades. A fuller understanding of kinship and family structures promised to shed light on naming procedures, just as the latter might reciprocally clarify the former.

The launching of large-scale studies of the imperial aristocracy (ninth to eleventh centuries) from the perspectives of prosopography, family structure, and descent practices at the Universities of Freiburg and Münster in the 1960s also led to intensive examination of naming practices. Then the publication and study of monastic necrologies, mainly Cluniac, from the tenth to twelfth centuries by members of the Münster school in the 1970s brought onomastics to the center of attention, for these texts contain almost nothing but thousands (often tens of thousands) of undifferentiated names never before carefully scrutinized and classified. Most recently a group of some twenty German scholars, both linguists and historians, has turned its attention to the huge mass of personal names surviving from the very early Middle Ages, one of the last great bodies of documentary sources for that period still relatively unexploited by modern medievalists. The subtitle of their project (located at the Universities of Duisburg, Saarbrücken, and Paderborn), "Nomen et Gens: The historical importance [or utility—*historische Aussagekraft*] of early medieval names," stresses their interest in the *historical* usefulness of a better understanding of these names and the ways they were attributed.[1]

Late in the 1980s a second movement got underway in France (in Tours, and more recently Paris) bringing together German, Spanish, Italian, and above all French historians in a project called "The Medieval Origins of Modern Naming" (La Genèse médiévale de l'anthroponymie moderne—GMAM). The accomplishments of this group, in range of

---

[1] *Nomen et gens: Zur historischen Aussagekraft frühmittelalterlichen Personennamen*, ed. Dieter Geuenich, Wolfgang Haubrichs, and Jörg Jarnut (Berlin, 1997). These are some of the papers presented at their first formal meeting as a group.

subjects examined, novelty of findings, and sheer volume of published results, have been exceptional. Between 1986 and 1995 it met seven times (1986, '87, '89, '90, '91, '93, '95) and then quickly published the proceedings in four volumes in 1990, '92, '95, and '97.[2] The subtitles of these collections give an idea of the scope of the subjects treated: the persistence of single names (for women, clerics, and in Brittany) well past the time of the introduction of second names in France in general; the use of statistical methods; genealogical inquiries; prosopography; and discussions of naming by contemporaries.

The enthusiasm engendered by the French undertaking led to the formation of a similar group comprised mainly of Italians but also including a number of French scholars for the study of naming practices in medieval Italy. Meetings took place in Rome in 1993, in Milan in 1994, and Rome again in 1997, and the École française de Rome published the *Acta* of these in 1994, '95, and '98.[3]

Finally representatives of both groups, French and Italian, came together along with German, Austrian, Spanish, and American colleagues, nearly forty in all, for an international colloquium in Rome in October 1994 on the theme of anthroponomy as an element in the social history of the Mediterranean world, taking into account Islamic/Arabic and Jewish populations as well as Christian.[4]

---

[2] *Genèse médiévale de l'anthroponymie moderne* (= GMAM). *I. Études d'anthroponymie médiévale Ie et IIe rencontres, Azay-le-Ferron 1986 et 1987*, ed. Monique Bourin (1990); GMAM, *II. Persistances du nom unique*, 1, *Le cas de la Bretagne. L'anthroponymie des clercs*, 2, *Désignation et anthroponymie des femmes. Méthodes statistiques pour l'anthroponymie*, ed. Monique Bourin and Pascal Chareille (1992); GMAM, *III. Enquêtes généalogiques et données prosopographiques*, ed. Monique Bourin and Pascal Chareille (1995); GMAM, *IV. Discours sur le nom: normes, usages, imaginaire (VIe–XVIe siècles)*, ed. Patrice Beck (1997).

[3] *Mélanges de l'École française de Rome. Moyen âge, temps modernes* (= MEFRM), 106/1 (1994), 106/2 (1995), and 110/1 (1998).

[4] *L'anthroponymie. Document de l'histoire sociale des mondes méditerranéens médiévaux*, ed. Monique Bourin, Jean-Marie Martin, and François Menant, Collections de l'École française de Rome 226 (Rome, 1996).

In retrospect the rapid succession of colloquia and published volumes in the 1990s amounts to nothing less than an explosion of activity by medieval historians on a subject that no one could have predicted as recently as 15 years ago. There can scarcely be any doubt that this represents one of the most vibrant, innovative, and productive movements in medieval scholarship at the present time.

But this overly mechanical recitation of Congresses and publications of the French/Italian *Genèse médiévale* groups has not yet come to an end, for the papers published in this collection are still another product of these scholars' research. Thirteen participants in the earlier meetings, ten French and three Spanish, assembled again in Kalamazoo in 1997 to present the results of their investigations as centered on a theme which has increasingly occupied specialists in name studies in recent times: relationships between personal naming practices and family structure. Rather than concentrating on one country or region during a single period, these essays range widely over the European scene from the Mediterranean—Portugal (1), Spain (3), Italy (2), and the French Midi (1), north to include France as a whole (2), and the Holy Roman Empire (1). A single paper examines crusader populations resettled in the Latin East. The essays likewise touch all periods of the Middle Ages though with a pronounced preference for the eleventh through thirteenth centuries; one author alone (Régine Le Jan) centers on the earlier centuries as does only one (Patrice Beck) for the later period. Most focus on naming among the aristocracy; Lluís To Figueras is an exception in dealing with peasants though the latter also enter into Beck's rural population.

Several of the contributors concentrated directly on the theme of the conference—naming and family history—but most touched on it tangentially as it related to the subjects of their individual presentations. Monique Bourin, co-organizer of this colloquium and coordinator of the *Genèse* movement since its beginnings, writes about "How Changes in Naming Reflect the Evolution of Familial Structures in Southern Europe 950–1250." She comes to the tentative conclusion that the two basic changes in naming from that period—(1), the increasing popularity of a

smaller number of different personal names, and (2), the triumph of a
two-element naming system (forename and surname) over the use of single
names alone—may have resulted less from the realignment of kinship
groups from a horizontal orientation to a vertical one centered around
agnatic lineages than from contemporary political developments, most
notably the spread of feudo-vassalic relations. Treating the early medieval
Frankish aristocracy (sixth to tenth centuries), Régine Le Jan has similar
reservations about the notion that the gradual abandonment of naming
through variation and its replacement through name repetition was due
mainly to the reorganization of groups of relatives from the horizontal to
the vertical multi-generational model. She maintains that at least in part
the preference for name repetition reflected new Christian ideas about
paternal authority in the conjugal family. In his study of northern Spain
in the High Middle Ages, Lluís To Figueras was struck by the fact that
peasants did not follow the aristocratic practice of turning to double
naming but adhered to the earlier custom of single names—because, he
concludes, lacking inheritance rights to the family patrimony they had less
interest in calling attention to their ancestors through a *nomen paternum*.
On the other hand Robert Durand found that the Portuguese aristocracy
clung to the use of the *nomen paternum* as the second name until the
fifteenth century with the result that the vertically-oriented lineage in which
the name of a single venerated male ancestor is repeated each generation
was not dominant in their society—at least as reflected in naming practices.

Italian onomastics in the central medieval period occupied the attention of François Menant—urban populations in the north—and Jean-
Marie Martin—the southern part of the peninsula and Sicily. While the
naming practices in the northern communal populations generally re-
sembled their counterparts in the rest of northwestern Europe, what
impressed Menant were the wide chronological variations between different towns and regions in the eventual adoption of hereditary surnames.
Martin, in his turn, noted that the combination of two-name elements
came to dominate much later in the south and in Sicily than in the north.
Studying naming in southern French society in the Midi at the same time,

Benoît Cursente found that the two-element system was firmly in place by 1100. He also concludes that to a significant degree naming in the Midi was influenced by the emergence of a new troubadour culture and the Occitan language. Investigating onomastics in France overall in the four-teenth and fifteenth centuries, Patrice Beck stresses the degree to which a uniform naming system gradually eliminated the regional variations of earlier times, a development in which Christian ideas about preferred saints' names played a significant role.

In contrast to their fellows, three of the group focused their attention not on naming in general but on specific sources in an effort to see what the latter could reveal about contemporary attitudes toward onomastic customs. Thus Joseph Morsel found surprisingly that inscriptions of lesser noble women's names on personal seals in thirteenth- and fourteenth-century Franconia differed significantly from the ways the same women were named in written documents. The three different historical/genea-logical texts Pascual Martínez Sopena scrutinized, from northern Spain from the twelfth to fourteenth centuries, generally confirmed the picture given by documentary sources of the evolution of aristocratic naming customs reflecting the emergence of vertically-oriented lineages. Her analysis of the *Lignages d'Outremer*, a genealogy of forty European families settled in the Holy Land and dating from the later thirteenth and early fourteenth centuries, led Marie-Adélaïde Nielen to the conclusion that the disruption caused by their move to a foreign land had little effect on the ways they named their children.

Carlos Laliena came to a similar conclusion with regard to the naming customs of the many French settlers in Aragon after the Reconquest of Muslim Saragossa early in the twelfth century. Initially they changed very little; thus their names stood out distinctly from those of the indigenous Aragonese—as did also those of the subject Muslim population which had chosen to stay on rather than move to the south.

Some purely methodological reflections by Pascal Chareille complete this collection with the recommendation that the historical study of naming be carried out simultaneously at macro and micro levels. Large-scale investigations involving the analysis of masses of names are essential for the correction of misimpressions left by unrepresentative small samples; but Chareille also shows how a micro-historical study can reveal that homonymy (different people bearing the same name) was less of a problem in a small village than suggested by reliance solely on figures on a global scale.

Viewed collectively these papers suggest certain tentative conclusions about the current state of the question in this relatively new historical approach to medieval onomastics. First, it is acknowledged that an essential precondition for further development is establishing the basic facts of naming practices for the different parts of the medieval world at all time periods—above all, dating as precisely as possible the decisive trends of the decline of single naming and the emergence of two-element naming, and noting the disappearance of once traditional names and the vogue for new ones. A number of the Kalamazoo papers were doing precisely this. A second necessity is the application of the comparative approach as also shown in these papers. Their authors could only see the particular significance of naming customs in their regions by knowing what the trends were in neighboring or distant places. Third, there is a danger of assuming that naming customs were uniform for all people at any given time: on the contrary, differences existed between males and females; between peasants and aristocracy; and between eldest sons and the younger ones. Finally, there is the importance of going beyond the raw onomastic data available in charters, contracts, and the like, to see what contemporaries thought about the assigning of names. In other words, medieval naming was a more complicated matter than might have been assumed: one of the most important accomplishments of the scholars in the *Genèse* group has been to show something of this complexity.

Historical (as opposed to linguistic) study of medieval onomastics has never thrived in North America, possibly because the mélange of names found here is drawn from so many different language backgrounds. A small but dedicated group of scholars animates a single journal specializing in the subject, *Names*, but this covers place- as well as personal names for all time periods and countries, and articles on medieval naming account for only a small part of its whole. I have never heard or read of personal name studies forming part of the graduate education of American medieval historians, or of any medievalist who ever taught the subject. The standard American reference work for the medieval period, *The Dictionary of the Middle Ages*,[5] from the 1980s, has no entry under "names," "personal names," "onomastics," or "toponomy," in contrast to the German *Lexikon des Mittelalters*,[6] also from the 1980s. One of the principal reasons for the organization of the Personal Names colloquium at the 1997 Kalamazoo Congress—the first time, to my knowledge, that onomastics has ever figured in a meeting of American medievalists—was to better acquaint our colleagues with one of the most fruitful fields of research in medieval scholarship at the present time.

GEORGE T. BEECH

---

[5]Joseph Reese Strayer, ed., *Dictionary of the Middle Ages* (New York, 1982).

[6]*Lexikon des Mittelalters*, 10 vols. (Munich, 1980–99).

PART I

METHODOLOGY

How Changes in Naming Reflect the Evolution of Familial Structures in Southern Europe (950–1250)

Monique Bourin

The present contribution is an introductory one and brings out some previously existing problems in the use of names for our knowledge of kinship. The problems with names studies are such that many questions remain unanswered, especially those that concern the links between personal names and the structures of kinship. At first glance, names appear plainly to be dictated by family policies, but the further we proceed in such a study, the less clear the leading principles of the policy appear. The hypothesis, believed to be simple at the outset, becomes blurred. At the level of the family, the reasons for the choice of given names may be varied; the social management of name choice is also submitted to complex rules.

Studies show that in a given region, at a given social level, naming practices are diverse. For example, the rigidity of the Guilhems de Montpellier stands in contrast with the relaxed policy of the Earls of Melgueil. The evolution of family naming policies is by no means a linear one. Personal names, consequently, make up an enormous body of material, difficult to interpret. It is easy to understand that it did not prove very attractive to historians, however heartily Marc Bloch[1] encouraged its study. After all, the conclusion may be that scholars who are keen on naming studies belong to a particularly masochistic species in their profession! Nonetheless, some of those historians have carried out anthroponymic

---

[1]Marc Bloch, "Noms de personne et histoire sociale," *Annales d'histoire économique et sociale* 4 (1932), 67, quoted in the introduction to Louis Pérouas et al., *Léonard, Marie, Jean et les autres. Les prénoms en Limousin depuis un millénaire* (Paris, 1984), p. 1.

research throughout Europe and their results can be summed up as follows here, simplifying to a high degree.

To begin with, regional differences were found to be very great, as the following papers will show, and they do not easily provide a clear view of the evolution of naming customs. There was also an overall evolution marked by the appearance of double naming. There was not a modification in the corpus of names, but there was a change in their distribution, with an increasing concentration on a few names, used more and more homogeneously throughout Europe. In other words, there was not so much an erosion of the repertoire as a concentration of choice on a few names. Most other names did not disappear, but did decline in popularity.[2] Represented graphically, the new distribution is bell-shaped and highly differentiated, becoming more and more elongated as time passes.

The second distinctive feature of the evolution of naming was the appearance of surnames, thus the use of two different names at the same time, with the surname gradually becoming a hereditary patronym.[3] Although the general features are rather easy to describe (though not always to explain), the micro-analysis at the level of individual families provides less clear results, at least until late into the thirteenth century, when the role played by spiritual kinship prevails, and hereditary transmission of surnames, even with exceptions, constitutes a fairly coherent system.

With regard to the evolution of kinship structures and their influence on personal names, a kind of general agreement has come to prevail among medievalists since the works of Karl Schmid and Georges Duby.[4] I cite

---

[2] On this point, see George Beech, "Les noms de personne poitevins du IXème au XIIème siècle," *Revue internationale d'onomastique* 26 (1974), 81–100.

[3] See *Genèse médiévale de l'anthroponymie moderne* (= GMAM), *I. Etudes d'anthroponymie médiévale Ie et IIe rencontres, Azay-le-Ferron 1986 et 1987,* ed. Monique Bourin (1990).

[4] Among some early studies about this topic, Karl Schmid, "Zur Problematik von Familie, Sippe und Geschlecht, Haus und Dynastie, beim mittelalterlichen Adel. Vorfragen zum Thema 'Adel und Herrschaft im Mittelalter'," *Zeitschrift für die Geschichte des Oberrheins* 105 (1957), 1–62; Georges Duby, "Structures de parenté et noblesse dans la France du

Martin Aurell[5] in a recent book on Western nobility: circa 1000, the lineage abruptly replaced the earlier, horizontally-constituted kinship, anchored on a castle, or around an estate, with descent traced through the male line and succession based on primogeniture. These are the distinctive features of that sudden transformation of kinship. This rapid transformation is conveyed in the changes in form of names given. There was a diffusion of the two-unit naming system, including the family patronym being associated with an individual first name, and this appears to be an innovation of aristocratic origin that was later extended to the whole of society from the early twelfth century. The system is simple, indeed far too simple, and regional studies have complicated the picture.

Two explanations, different as they seem to be, have been advanced to account for the appearance of surnames. The first explanation is that the surname became necessary because of an increasing homonymy, that is, too many different people bore the same name. The second is that the surname, as transmitted through the male line, was the onomastic image of the new lineage.

The argument invoking homonymy is not totally satisfactory, at least as far as being the principal factor in the process. It is an example of a good idea that proves to be wrong! It is clear that the classical explanation can be reversed and that one can argue that the appearance of surnames allowed an increasing number of individuals to bear the same, highly-regarded first name. Homonymy and surnames work, in that case, within a spiral process of simultaneous development. Therefore, without giving it up completely, it is more logical to discard homonymy as a primary cause in the evolution of the naming system. Let us instead try to find out if the two processes—new choices in naming and advent of surnames—cannot correspond to a similar evolution of kinship structures.

Nord aux XIème et XIIème siècles," in *Hommes et structures du Moyen Age* (Paris, 1973), pp. 267–85.

[5]Martin Aurell, *La noblesse en Occident (Ve–XVe siècle)* (Paris, 1996), pp. 64–65.

Actually, the consensus regarding the evolution of kinship structures is more apparent than real. Recently, the idea of any radical evolution in the eleventh century has gone out of vogue. Speaking of revolution, or even of mutation, has, in a very brief period of time, become quite unfashionable.[6] Nowadays medievalists speak of gradual modification instead of abrupt changes. Should a similar reconsideration be applied to naming? Should we discard the concept of a revolution in naming? At the same time, if it is naming that has brought to light this evolution of kinship structures, then the question of the evolution of kinship structures must itself be reexamined, and the notion of a sudden transformation rejected—if it is, in fact, the case that it is naming that has brought the evolution to light, for it has not yet been ascertained that the two curves are perfectly parallel.

Anthropologists such as Jack Goody[7] are not as certain as historians are that the changes in naming are to be interpreted as a regrouping of the lineage and as a proof of its agnatic character. On this point they are followed by such historians as Michael Mitterauer.[8] In fact, they have found that the system according to which a name was passed down through alternate generations, mainly from grandfather to eldest grandson, was abandoned, at least partially. In most of the places where that system was to be found, it points to ancestor worship and to a belief in the possibility of the transmission of the spiritual elements of personality. According to Goody, the choice of names by godparents was the decisive factor, as

---

[6]After the controversial book of Guy Bois, *La mutation de l'an mil* (Paris, 1989), see Dominique Barthélemy, *La mutation de l'an mil a-t-elle eu lieu? Servage et chevalerie dans la France des Xe et XIe siècles* (Paris, 1997). For a broad approach to the different points of view, see the debate published by *Past and Present*, involving Thomas N. Bisson, Stephen White, Timothy Reuter, Dominique Barthélemy, and Chris Wickham.

[7]Jack Goody, *The Development of the Family and Marriage in Europe* (Cambridge, 1983).

[8]Michael Mitterauer, *Ahnen und Heilige. Namengebung in der europäischen Geschichte* (Munich, 1993).

Michael Bennett[9] thought, and, with regard to the naming of children, spiritual kinship prevailed over blood relationships.

The hypothesis is an interesting one but it poses problems. First of all, it has to be proved that names of spiritual kin in fact suddenly began to make deep inroads in naming around 1000. Actually, as was pointed out earlier, there is no such evidence prior to the late thirteenth century. This kind of a naming system does not appear to have been firmly established before the fourteenth century. The hypothesis of a shrinkage in the variety of names due to the establishment of a strict system of transmission is an interesting one, but it does not appear to have been linked exclusively to the introduction of the names of spiritual kin.

In any case, these analyses suggest that changes in the popularity of names (name distribution) can be interpreted as resulting from a deliberate rejection of earlier naming customs, or, as Patrick Geary[10] has argued, from the management of familial memory. It is therefore essential to check the modalities carefully, not only in a quantitative but also in a qualitative way. The transformation of names, perceptible on a large scale, must also express familial choices. Was there slow, continuous evolution or sudden, radical change? After the adoption of new names, was it a question of establishing a new stock of family names to be handed down to affect all the children, all of whom would receive names drawn from this new stock, or were certain children—the eldest son, for instance—exempted from it? In this case, the elder children would have become the bearers of the family tradition and the changes in naming would have gone along with a differentiation in the ranks of the children and the emergence of a kind of

[9]Michael Bennett, "Spiritual Kinship and the Baptismal Name in Traditional European Society," in *Principalities, Powers and Estates. Studies in Medieval and Modern Government and Society*, ed. L. O. Frappell (Adelaide, 1979), pp. 1–13. For a different opinion about the influence of spiritual kinship, see Joseph H. Lynch, *Godparents and Kinship in Early Medieval Europe* (Princeton, 1986).

[10]Patrick Geary, *Living with the Dead in the Middle Ages* (Ithaca, 1994); Geary, *La mémoire et l'oubli à la fin du premier millénaire*, trans. Jean-Pierre Ricard (Paris, 1996), pp. 83–128.

primogeniture. Did the break affect all of the members of a family or did it exclude some of the children, especially the eldest? In that case, they would be the bearers of the family memory, and the break would keep pace with a new affirmation of a discrimination among the children, establishing a kind of primogeniture.[11]

The answer to such questions is far from simple, given the difficulties in evaluating whether an evolution is the spontaneous dynamic of a stock of names, or the forerunner of a real change. Before advancing further in the interpretation of naming data with regard to kinship structures, especially with regard to tightening or relaxing their constraint, it is important to remember that they have to be approached in several ways, some of which have been neglected by medievalists: first, the evolution of the vocabulary of kinship, and second, an analysis of the type of affectivity prevailing in families. The data from literature have been partly explored, but wills must also be studied, as well as choice of burial place, bequests of clothes, and other tenuous though important marks of feeling, as far as family is concerned.

Those approaches are indispensable for completing the research thus far carried out, that is, the devolution of patrimonial goods and the genealogical management of names. The devolution of patrimonial goods has mostly been studied through legal texts, and mostly customary ones, but it has yet to be shown how these worked in practice.

Constructions of genealogies are necessary, but these turn out to be a deceptive "metasource" for many reasons. Because a genealogical table induces the false impression that individuals mentioned in it bear a single surname, it simulates a "family name" at a time when such an appellation had not yet come into use. Also, a transmitted name catches the eye and exaggerates its importance in the actual devolution of names. After reviewing a great many genealogies, one is struck in fact by the scarcity of cases, aside from exceptions, in which the same name is to be found, in the same

---

[11] *L'anthroponymie. Document de l'histoire sociale des mondes méditerranéens médiévaux*, ed. Monique Bourin, Jean-Marie Martin, and François Menant (Rome, 1996), pp. 365–433.

family, during more than three generations. The biological misfortune of an eldest son and bearer of such a "patrimonial" name who died without heirs is often not balanced by the re-establishment of this name in a junior branch of the family. Great families excepted, the commitment to an onomastic patrimony is not so obvious as is commonly thought.

In addition, genealogy—based on the data of charters—presents a system more agnatic than kinship structures actually are. Charters mention land insofar as it is connected to power, and female persons are normally omitted. Women are not especially poor, as they are not excluded from the kin, but charters are rather little acquainted with their names and, even less, with their family origins.

A still more important consideration is that genealogies, such as it is the historian's duty to reconstitute them, suggest long-term memory that was probably by no means the common type of memory at those times. The modern reconstitution of genealogies may attribute a long stability to family names which is artificial or false. It may have been the case that there was a succession of three generational segments that overlap one another, for example. Interrupting a tradition of three generations does not have the same meaning as interrupting a long sequence of generations.

It is the historian's task to reconstitute genealogies as a metasource with the utmost erudition; they are an unavoidable preliminary to the intelligibility of family structures,[12] but they require caution so as not to lead to attractive, but ill-founded, interpretations.

Notwithstanding the reservations expressed here, can names give access to knowledge of kinship structures? I shall confine myself to two sets of remarks, based on a few specific examples and on some large-scale considerations. This will lead to some rather pessimistic comments.

The agnatic transmission of surnames is, no doubt, an established fact—whatever the system is, *nomen paternum* or some other. Matronyms

---

[12]See, as a good example, Claudie Duhamel-Amado, "La famille aristocratique langedocienne. Parenté et patrimoine dans les vicomtés de Béziers et d'Agde" (Ph.D. diss., University of Paris IV, 1994); and *Genèse des lignages méridionaux* (Toulouse, 2001).

are exceptions and reflect particular circumstances. In the same way, it does appear that the names of children are more often inspired by the corpus of the paternal branch, except in case of hypergamy. But is this really a new practice? An analysis of the transmission of onomastic themes in Carolingian polyptics shows that paternal themes influence them more than maternal ones, even when female children are concerned. If there was an evolution, it had very old roots.[13]

Does the choice of names reveal the existence of a clearly organized grouping of brothers and sisters, or the strict organization of a brother-hood? Does it reveal the application of new principles of primogeniture and exclusion of female members? It seems that there is a link between methods of naming and organization of siblings for the Iberian countries, where the *nomen paternum* system persistently pursues its course, and that it also presents the principle of parity between all the children born in the same generation.[14] It remains to be determined, in countries where this system co-exists with others, whether it is correlated, at a family level, with the maintenance of egalitarian inheritance.

What are the conditions in other countries? First, there is the question of female exclusion. In fact, in the charters, women seldom bear a surname; they are designated by their name followed by a family relationship, wife or daughter most of the time.[15] On the one hand, what is valid for charters is not valid for epigraphy or heraldry. On the other hand, in charters, the fact is clearer and more persistent, and even more so when a woman is in a high social position. Finally, the chronological data should

---

[13]Hans-Werner Goetz, "Zur Namengebung bäuerlichen Schichten im Frühmittelalter. Untersuchungen und Berechnungen anhand des Polyptichons von Saint-Germain-des-Prés," *Francia* 15 (1987), 852–77.

[14]*Antroponimia y sociedad. Sistemas de identificación hispano-cristianos en los siglos IX a XIII*, ed. Pascual Martínez Sopena (Santiago de Compostella-Valladolid, 1995).

[15]There is a huge literature about this topic; on the specific problem of female naming, see GMAM, *II. Persistance du nom unique. 2, Désignation et anthroponymie des femmes. Méthodes statistiques pour l'anthroponymie*, ed. Monique Bourin and Pascal Chareille (1992).

be checked in every case. In Languedoc, as soon as children begin to be named in the charters, circa 1000, daughters are grouped after sons. Change in chancellery habits seems to predate stages in the evolution of naming and inheritance customs.

Do the choices of names confirm the fact of female exclusion? The dominance of a few preferred female names comes probably somewhat later than for men, but we must recognize that these calculations are based on small samples. It is puzzling that the main evolution in the twelfth century continued to be, as it was in the era of Charlemagne, the creation of female names taken from the male names predominant at the time, for instance *Guillelma* or *Johanna*.

The naming system of primogeniture took a long time to take root. In Languedoc, the identical repetition of a name from the father to the eldest son does not occur as a rule before the late thirteenth century.[16] This is not, I suspect, a peculiarity of Languedoc. In society as a whole, the devolution of names gradually created a special place for the eldest son.

Thus, in both fields, it is the slow, gradual evolution of naming practices that is the striking feature. The names changed, but the principles of family naming did not. One should check, case after case, in the families where it is possible to reveal it, whether the devolution of patrimonial goods and names really keep pace with one another.

Is the emergence of surnames based on the lineage a sign of a growing family consciousness and tighter constraints? This is doubtless true. However, it is not certain that the extent of family memory is to be judged by the date of surname constitution; rather, the contrary is true. Portuguese genealogies go back as far as genealogical histories of great families

---

[16]Monique Bourin, "Tels pères, tels fils? L'héritage du nom dans la noblesse languedocienne (XIème–XIIIème siècles)," in GMAM, *III. Enquêtes généalogiques et données prosopographiques*, ed. Monique Bourin and Pascal Chareille (1995), pp. 191–210; and about the problem in general of the choices in naming among the Languedoc nobility, see Duhamel-Amado, "La famille," pp. 435–605.

bearing an eponymous castral surname.[17] Furthermore, close observation based on a prosopographical study, above all in noble families, shows that the surname based on the lineage is far from being an early phenomenon. It changes more than it appears in the space of a few generations; two brothers do not systematically take the same surname, even if one of them, and not always the elder, bears the name of his father.

The uncertainty and gradual character of this evolution lead to a fundamental question: are these changes in naming resulting from changes in family structures?

It does not seem to me as though, within the Mediterranean world, there is a clear relationship between the forms and rhythm of evolution in naming and those concerning the organization of patrimonial goods. This is all the more true with regard to kinship structures. An early emergence of the family surname does not appear to directly correlate to changes in inheritance practices, though it fits in with the *laudatio parentum* fairly well.

The evolution in naming seems to follow two different rhythms depending on one's point of observation. At the level of the family, there is a slow, uncertain tempo but more clearly visible if seen on a broader scale, for names are also submitted to social control and not just to that of the family. In certain countries, the change was radical. It may be argued that the rigidity of certain chancelleries in their sudden desire to update naming practices played a role. But it does not seem to me that such an argument explains the slowness of Italy in converting to two-unit names and the contrasting rapidity of Catalonia[18] or Languedoc, both of which embraced them for nearly all the population.

---

[17]Robert Durand, "Trois siècles de dénomination aristocratique portugaise d'après la littérature généalogique," in GMAM III, ed. Bourin and Chareille (1995), pp. 43–54.

[18]See Michel Zimmermann, "Les débuts de la révolution anthroponymique en Catalogne XIème–XIIème siècles" and Lluís To Figueras, "Antroponimia de los condados catalanes (Barcelona, Girona y Osuna, siglos X–XIII)," in *Antroponimia y sociedad,* ed. Martínez Sopena, pp. 351–94.

That is why it is my impression, however paradoxical it may seem, that the broad outline of the evolution in naming is mainly the sign of socio-political changes, the rhythms of which are not exactly those of the economy and kinship structures. Are not the rapidity and profundity of the onomastic evolution in Catalonia or Languedoc in perfect accord with a time of rapid and profound feudalization? Would not the long-term survival at Pisa[19] of names based on complementary designation be the sign of a land little affected by feudalism? Were one to ask me what I mean by feudalization, I hope I would be allowed to answer that the question would really lead us too far astray.

---

[19]On the Italian naming system, see *Mélanges de l'Ecole française de Rome* 106 (1994) and 107 (1995), 427–66. The latter contains a specific study of the Pisan case by Enrica Salvatori entitled "Il sistema antroponimico a Pisa nel Duecento: la citta e il territorio."

METHODOLOGICAL PROBLEMS IN A QUANTITATIVE APPROACH TO CHANGES IN NAMING

Pascal Chareille

Every paper in this volume stresses the complex nature of the relationships between personal names and kinship structures in medieval society. I would like to draw attention to some of the specific methodological problems raised by personal name studies, particularly in the context of transformations in the individual naming system and family structures.

For the specialist of the Middle Ages, the study of personal names is generally based on data provided by the more or less homogenous, often sketchy or incomplete, mass of documentation. These data permit the study of only a certain number of individuals out of the population on which the historian bases his investigations, and so he cannot hope to apprehend anything more than a partial reality. Studies undertaken in different European countries—over roughly the past ten years, in the context of the program on the medieval genesis of modern anthroponomy—are no exception to this rule.

The breadth of this collective survey and the quantitative approach adopted necessitated the implementation of a specific methodology and the use of appropriate statistical indicators. We can imagine the constraints imposed by such an undertaking. As far as possible, each researcher has had to adhere to rules for the perusal of his sources, use analytical grids and typologies, and have recourse to a certain number of indicators in order to describe the corpus. Some of the very first methodologies proposed have had to be abandoned while others have survived, either supplemented or adapted in order to provide a response to the ever-increasing number of questions raised by the different types of documents.

The Macro-Analytical Level

The statistical tools that have allowed us to outline the evolution that led to the setting up of a system of two-element naming, in a form and at a rate that are better known and understood today,[1] have been developed in the macro-analytical perspective. In fact, previous studies have so far been centered on a global analysis of the evolution of the system. Within this framework, the instruments in current use have allowed historians to show the following: the appearance of the surname was not necessarily due to a correlation between the concentration of the choice of names, and a possible risk of homonymy; the phenomenon took place at a very variable rate; males who were not members of the clergy were the first to use the new system; and the socially differentiated analysis of anthroponymic behaviors was complex. It would seem that there are several reasons for this deep-seated change in naming: new and greater affirmation of religious belief, new frameworks of political and parish organization, and new family structures.[2] It is difficult to establish a hierarchy of the various reasons, however, and many questions remain unanswered.

---

[1] *Genèse médiévale de l'anthroponymie moderne* (= GMAM), ed. Monique Bourin (Tours, 1990); GMAM, *II. Persistances du nom unique*. 1, *Le cas de la Bretagne, l'anthroponymie des clercs*; and 2, *Désignation et anthroponymie des femmes. Méthodes statistiques pour l'anthroponymie*, ed. Monique Bourin and Pascal Chareille (Tours, 1992); GMAM, *III. Enquêtes généalogiques et données prosopographiques*, ed. Monique Bourin and Pascal Chareille (Tours, 1995); *L'anthroponymie. Document de l'histoire sociale des mondes méditerranéens médiévaux*, ed. Monique Bourin, Jean-Marie Martin, and François Menant (Rome, 1996); GMAM, *L'espace italien. Mélanges de l'École française de Rome. Moyen âge, temps modernes* (= MEFRM), 106/2 (Rome, 1994), ed. Jean-Marie Martin and François Menant, pp. 313–736; GMAM, *L'espace italien*. MEFRM 107/2 (Rome, 1995), ed. Jean-Marie Martin and François Menant, pp. 331–633; *Antroponimia y sociedad. Sistemas de identificacion hispano-cristianos en los siglos IX a XIII*, ed. Pascual Martínez Sopena (Santiago de Compostella-Valladolid, 1995); GMAM, *IV. Discours sur le nom: normes, usages, imaginaire (VIe–XVIe siècles)*, ed. Patrice Beck (Tours, 1997).

[2] This last point contains a particularly complex issue. In her paper, Bourin emphasizes the fact that changes in personal naming are not necessarily the sign of a transformation in family structures.

The construction of statistical indicators capable of giving an objective account of the modalities and rhythms of the changes is no easy task. These indicators must permit regional, chronological and social comparisons, even where there is a possible lack of unity in the documentation. They must be "robust." By this I mean that they must remain indifferent to variations in certain parameters that may be difficult to control. They must also permit the evaluation of the validity of results for samples, which may be quite small, concerning certain regions, periods of time, or social categories. Statisticians tend to consider analyses based on samples of fewer than thirty occurrences as belonging in this category. It will be realized that this sort of situation is quite common in the field of medieval studies. This cannot be achieved without recourse to suitable statistical analytical procedures, which may sometimes lead to the invalidation of certain preliminary results.

As far as macro-analysis is concerned, the most efficacious tool for the study of names appears to be the establishment by time periods and social categories of a "hit-parade of names." This hit-parade will give us the number and distribution of names according to the number of people who bear them. A certain number of specific statistical indicators prove useful in characterizing this distribution.[3] We may classify them according to the type of information they provide about the corpus, and the conscious or unconscious use that the group makes of this information:

I. The condensation of the corpus, evaluated by the average number of individuals per name, or its equivalent, the stock of names for 100 individuals.

II. The concentration of the corpus, evaluated by:

A. the proportion of individuals designated by the five most commonly used names;

B. the minimum number of names necessary (and sufficient) to designate at least half the individuals; and

---

[3]A detailed presentation of these indicators can be found in Pascal Chareille's "Éléments pour un traitement statistique des données anthroponymiques," in GMAM II.2, pp. 245–97.

C.   the global concentration index, associated with the curve of concentration of distribution.[4] This index is equal to zero (minimum value) when all the individuals have different names; it is equal to one (maximum value) when all the individuals have the same name.

III.   The extension of the corpus, evaluated by:
    A.   the number of different names; and
    B.   the number and proportion of names appearing only once in the sample, and the number and proportion of individuals who can be designated by these names.

IV.   The rate of homonymy in the corpus, evaluated by the probability that two individuals, picked out of a group at random, will have the same name. This probability is equal to zero (minimum value) if all the names in the corpus are different; it is equal to one (maximum value) if the names are all identical.

There may be risks attached to the use of these parameters. We therefore need to point out certain biases. It is very difficult, for example, to suggest a really efficacious method of measuring the condensation of the stock of names because of the obvious correlation between sample size and the value of the parameter. Condensation (stock of names for one hundred individuals) obviously increases with the size of the sample on which the analysis is based. This may make comparisons difficult, especially between groups of different sizes. Condensation will increase independently of any other factor[5] if the analysis is based on a number of occurrences greater than the number of available names (the latter number, while unknown, cannot be infinite).

Other, more insidious biases are more directly linked to the problem, and refer us to more vast historical questions. For example, it is well

---

[4]This curve (Lorenz type) shows the proportion of individuals designated by a given percentage of names in the corpus.

[5]This does not mean that it is impossible to compare condensation between two samples of different sizes, but an *ad hoc* statistical procedure must be implemented.

known that in order to explain the appearance of the surname and thus the establishment of a two-element naming system, historians have long put forward the idea of a more or less progressive depletion of the corpus of names, with its consequent effects upon homonymy. This hypothesis does not stand up to careful theoretical examination. Two points, at least, must be emphasized in this connection.

First, it is very hard to be affirmative as far as the erosion of the stock of names is concerned. For a given region and time period, it is not at all easy to know the number and the exact distribution of names according to the number of people who bear them. No "sampling" in the statistical sense of the word will give us a satisfactory estimate of this distribution. The complex nature of the problem, for which there is no simple theoretical solution, stems from the fact that, while estimates of the occurrences of the most common names in the population studied can easily be made from data provided by the samples (and extrapolated to the whole of the population), the same is not at all true for rare names (names given to a small number of individuals). There is very little likelihood that a name that is rarely found in the population of a given region will show up in a sample.

The graph on the next page, which is the result of the construction of a model of the problem, demonstrates this point. It shows the probability (values of ordinates) for different sizes of samples (values of abscissas) of a name borne by a given fraction (values in margin) of the population actually appearing in the sample.

Thus, there is slightly more than a 20 percent chance that a name borne by only five individuals in one thousand (5 p. 1000) in the population of reference will appear in a sample of fifty. A name borne by fewer than 2 percent (2 p. 100) has a likelihood of less than 50 percent of appearing in a sample of thirty. We can clearly see that when names are borne by a small number of individuals (fewer than one per thousand), the probability of their appearing in a sample of two hundred is very low, whereas in actual fact, many studies base their findings on those sorts of numbers.[6]

---

[6]They refer to figures available for periods of time; the total number of occurrences of names is, generally, greater than two hundred.

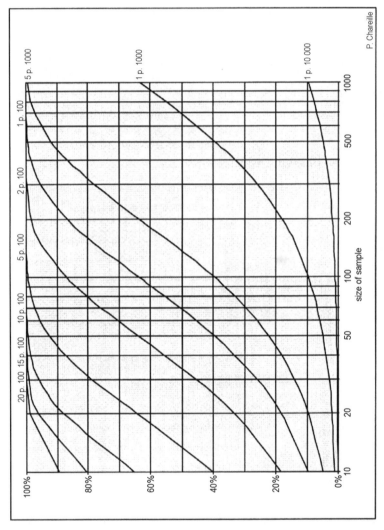

Abacus of names "lost from documentation"

P. Chareille

The necessarily rigorous verification of the possible erosion of the corpus of names, like its possible renewal, can only be envisaged in the light of very complete documentation, or at the least, of very large samples. Few medieval collections allow such an approach, especially over any great length of time. Careful observation of those sources that provide exceptional amounts of information on personal names[7] shows that the number of different names would seem to have remained very large throughout the Middle Ages (and not simply, as has often been suggested, during the earlier periods) and that names borne by a single individual make up a large part of the corpus of names (often more than half), even though the concentration of choice on certain names was greater during this period.

This concentration of choices on certain names must not, however, be interpreted as going necessarily hand in hand with an erosion of the stock, which might be a cause or a consequence of this concentration. We can also understand better that, in the absence of sufficiently large samples, some regional studies might have given the mistaken impression that there is a perpetual renewal of the corpus.

Second, the measure of homonymy, or the probability that two individuals picked out of the same group at random will have the same name, is not to be confused with the more or less dense concentration of choice on certain names. The most commonly found name can designate nearly one out of four individuals and the rate of homonymy in the corresponding population be no more than 6 percent. This is true of Metz in the fourteenth century, for example.[8] A similar result can be found for Florence

---

[7]Such sources include the polyptychs of Saint-Germain-des-Prés and of Saint-Victor de Marseille for the early Middle Ages, and the registers of the Paris *taille* and Florentine tax registers for the later periods, and there are others. The anthroponymic material has been taken from published work or from work in progress. At the time we write, the corresponding detailed statistical studies have not yet been published.

[8]The anthroponymic data analyzed are those of the cartulary of the Petit-Clairvaux of Metz (men only, $n = 1943$). They were taken from computerized files supplied by Patricia Dreyfus, "Étude du système anthroponymique de la ville de Metz au XIVe siècle d'après le cartulaire du Petit-Clairvaux de Metz" (Ph.D. diss., University of Paris I, 1996).

in the fifteenth century, where the two most commonly found names designate more than 15 percent of individuals, with a rate of homonymy of only 2.7 percent.[9]

We have numerous examples in which the rate of homonymy remains relatively low, while the most common names designate nearly 20 percent of all individuals. This is an important point, inasmuch as it implies that neither the usual parameters of concentration—the proportion of individuals designated by the five most common names or the number of names needed to designate half the individuals in the group, nor even the parameters of condensation (the average number of individuals per name, or stock of names for 100 individuals)—will allow us to account satisfactorily for this homonymy.

It must also be said that this notion is only meaningful, or more precisely is only operational, at a certain level of observation, and hence of analysis. The elements previously presented concern macroanalysis. The "acceptability threshold," as far as homonymy is concerned, is doubtless not the same within a village community, a region, or a family.

More generally, we can only talk in a meaningful way of the concentration or of the dispersion of names, of the rate of homonymy or the rhythm of evolution, with reference to a given scale of observation. Some of the statistical parameters used to describe the corpus may be more sensitive to the way the instruments of measurement are adjusted than they are to the real variation in the "object of study." Personal name studies are no different from any of the other social sciences in this respect. We know that this problem exists in many areas. It may even have led to a certain loss of interest in quantitative historical studies. In any case, it is certainly at the heart of the theoretical reflection on scales of observation which was started several years ago by "micro-history."[10]

---

[9]The anthroponymic data analyzed, which were kindly furnished by Christiane Klapisch-Zuber, are those of the 1427 Catasto of Florence (men only, n = 9910).

[10]Jacques Revel, *Jeux d'échelles. La micro-analyse à l'expérience* (Paris, 1996).

In the field of personal name studies, as Monique Bourin has demonstrated (and here I am only repeating her argument), there are at least two levels of observation: the global level, or that of macro-analysis, which seems to be characterized by brutal changes; and the family level, or that of micro-analysis, in which the changes in personal naming are, to some extent, still not entirely clear to us.

The Micro-Analytical Level

How do these two levels co-exist? Are the transformations of the naming system, which we can perceive at the scale of macro-analysis, expressed at the family level? Can minor changes at the family level lead to major changes at a global level? The system we start to see established towards the end of the eleventh century appears to be more flexible than the contemporary naming system. In some families it would seem that the surname becomes partially hereditary very early on, at least over several generations and for certain children. In other families it will, for a long time, very definitely be attached to individuals. The institution of a patronymic (i.e., strictly hereditary) system took place at both a regional and a social level, at a pace and in a form that require further examination.

In order to answer the questions raised by a change in the scale of observation, it is necessary to deploy new instruments. It is clear, in fact, that if we want to analyze the working of the personal name system in the family, we must adopt appropriate tools and indicators that will be capable of measuring, for instance, the hereditary transfer of naming elements. Moreover, the transmission of a name or a surname to one child is not at all the same thing as the systematic passing down of a name or surname to all the children in a phratry. Concerning the family, we must differentiate two levels of analysis: that of analysis "as a family" and that of analysis "as individuals." This will allow us to differentiate between "names of lines" and "family names."

While new indicators may be used, some of the tools proposed for a global analysis can still be used for a micro-analysis. This is the case, for example, with the "hit-parade of names." A careful study of the hit-parade, analyzed family by family, should reveal whether the most common names in a given region or period of time are also those most frequently used as family markers. There is no reason why this should be the case. We can perfectly well imagine the existence of a small number of names that illustrate the renown of certain families. These names may be commonly found in the families concerned, but quite rarely elsewhere. Other names might be chosen, alongside these characteristic names, out of what would be a vast corpus. These are obviously merely hypotheses. Many other models can be envisaged.[11]

The distribution of rare names also needs to be specified. Do some families show a greater concentration of rare names than others? Are these names to be found alongside names that refer to the families' renown? In what conditions? Some names are seemingly reserved for certain children: what exactly is the situation? Is there a differentiation according to birth rank? Should we talk of determinism in the choice of names? These are all questions that deserve quantified answers.

The *experimental* analysis at two levels of observation (macro and micro) of several Vendôme genealogies[12] (which admittedly do not represent a very extensive source since the counts that have been taken concern only twenty-five noble genealogies comprising approximately five hundred people, and could in no way be felt to provide any definite answers to the above questions) shows, first, that as far as certain families are concerned, it is impossible to define names that authentically refer to family renown in any way; second, that names that often refer to family renown are not necessarily the most commonly found names in the "hit-parade," even if this is so in more than half the cases; third, that up to the thirteenth

---

[11]Bringing out the specificity of such models does suppose, however, that we have at our disposal enough information about each family, and hence a wealth of genealogical data, that probably nobility alone can provide.

[12]The anthroponymic material of these (noble) genealogies was taken from Dominique Barthélemy, *La société dans le comté de Vendôme: de l'an mil au XIVe siècle* (Paris, 1993).

century at least, the transmission of names appears to be more frequent than that of surnames (though it is not possible, in the present state of our knowledge, to identify the true models of devolution), even in those families where we do find the hereditary passing down of surnames; and lastly, that certain families would appear to resort more readily than others to the use of rare names, but it is not possible for us to say whether a correlation exists between this practice and the number or type of names referring to family renown.

We must be aware of the remarkable nature of the chosen corpus. The experiment must, of course, be extended to other classes and especially, wherever sources will allow, beyond the aristocracy, perhaps as far as the minor nobility, or even the well-to-do peasantry. This obviously depends on our ability to overcome the difficulties linked to the probable paucity of the information available about these populations. However that may be, the methodological approach is more important than the result obtained on this particular corpus. It should permit us to find objective answers to several of the fundamental questions posed by the change in scale of observation.

Finally, we may ponder the consequences on the stock of names—in terms of concentration, for example—of the setting up of a strict system of devolution of names or of surnames in the family group. Is it possible that the concentration of choices originates in such a system? This question deserves to be examined theoretically, since it is one that cannot be resolved by multiplying case studies. A model of the process must be constructed (as, for example, can be done for the process of extinction of current family names),[13] but the parameters to be taken into account in order for this to be achieved are numerous and hard to control. Supposing

---

[13]There are many theoretical studies on this subject. See, for example, Nicolas Brouard, *L'extinction des noms de famille en France: une approche*, Dossiers et Recherches 27 (Paris, 1989); or for a less technical presentation, Jacques Dupâquier and Denis Kessler, "Nos patronymes vont-ils disparaître?," in Jacques Dupâquier and Denis Kessler, eds., *La Société française au XIXe siècle* (Paris, 1992), 461–88.

that spiritual kinship plays a very important part in the devolution of names (this hypothesis is often put forward, for later periods at least), the construction of a model must enable us to follow, starting from a given initial state, the consequences of such a process on the stock of names over succeeding generations.

Conclusion

In writing this paper, we aimed to draw attention to some specific problems of methodology raised by medieval personal name studies rather than systematically explaining the solutions that have been proposed to overcome the difficulties. Certain questions still remain unanswered; it will probably prove necessary to construct certain statistical tools. But it seems to us that certain fundamental points need to be stressed.

First, while the multiplication of the number of case studies is necessary for an understanding of the logic behind the different systems of hereditary names and the breaks in personal naming patterns, it can in no way take the place of a broader, more theoretical reflection and, particularly, of the construction of models for certain processes.

Second, the reflection on the scale of observation, in particular, is absolutely fundamental. Macro-analysis (we refer here to the analysis of personal naming at the level of a social group, time period or region) is no substitute for micro-analysis (we refer here to the analysis of personal naming at a family level). The opposite is also true.

Third, there is no such thing as an instrument of measurement that is unlikely to be affected, one way or another, by variations in the scale of observation.

Fourth, there is no contradiction between illustrating the existence of a super-structure and that of a simpler structure, by which I mean valid at a lower level of observation. Each level of analysis is necessary, but neither is sufficient by itself. Moreover, it is by no means certain that the one will enable a perfect understanding of the other. This does not mean, either, that the two levels of analysis will necessarily lead to incompatible conclusions. It is possible in theory, at least, for the family approach to lead to results that hardly match those that a global approach will give.

Last, the coherence (or unity) of the results at each level of analysis is not guaranteed. This has to be established in every case.

Whatever the level of observation studied, making an objective account of the evolutions in anthroponymic practice is a complex matter. Many historical problems remain; one reason is that the methodological tools we have at our disposal provide results that are often not easily interpreted. Historians are necessarily led to ask themselves questions, not only about the nature of the information revealed by personal name study, which is an exercise in the critical study of documents to which they are well accustomed, but they must also reflect on the validity or the specificity of certain statistical results. This is an exercise with which they are doubtless much less familiar.

PART II

PERSONAL NAMES IN THE EARLY MIDDLE AGES

PERSONAL NAMES AND THE TRANSFORMATION OF KINSHIP IN EARLY MEDIEVAL SOCIETY (SIXTH TO TENTH CENTURIES)

Régine Le Jan[1]

From the sixth century onward, the Germanic custom of using only one name was standard in early medieval society.[2] This system of naming was not abandoned until the eleventh to twelfth centuries, when the use of the *nomen paternum* and of the surname became common.[3]

---

[1] I would like to thank Julia H. Smith for translating this article and for her comments.

[2] Henry Bosley Woolf, *The Old Germanic Principles of Name-Giving* (Baltimore, 1939); Henning Kaufmann, *Ergänzungsband zu Ernst Förstemann, altdeutsche Personennamen* (Munich, 1968); and Benno Eide Siebs, *Die Personennamen der Germanen* (Wiesbaden, 1970).

[3] A large-scale project on personal names was begun in Germany early in the 1970s by Karl Schmid, "Personenforschung und Namenforschung am Beispiel der Klostergemeinschaft von Fulda," *Frühmittelalterliche Studien* 5 (1971), 235–67, and Dieter Geuenich, "Vorbemerkungen zu einer philologischen Untersuchung frühmittelalterlicher Personennamen," in *Alemannica, Landeskundliche Beiträge. Festschrift für Bruno Boesch* (Bühl/Baden, 1976), pp. 118–42. Rudolf Schützeichel gave a preliminary historiographical summary in 1986, "Zur Namenforschung," *Beiträge zur Namenforschung* 21 (1986), 1–13. On the general evolution and transformation of ways of naming see Michael Mitterauer, *Ahnen und Heilige. Namengebung in der europäische Geschichte* (Munich, 1993). On naming among the Franks in the early Middle Ages, see Régine Le Jan, *Famille et pouvoir dans le monde franc (VIIe–Xe siècle). Essai d'anthropologie sociale* (Paris, 1995). On the appearance of the *nomen paternum* and the surname, see Monique Bourin, *Genèse de l'anthroponymie moderne* (= GMAM), particularly volume 1 (Tours, 1990). See also Bourin and Chareille's GMAM, *II. Persistances du nom unique* (Tours, 1992). Similarly, see GMAM, *L'espace italien. Mélanges de l'École française de Rome. Moyen âge, temps modernes* (= MEFRM), ed. Jean-Marie Martin and François Menant (1995).

In the course of the period between the sixth and tenth centuries, the hereditary transmission of names gradually spread from the top to the bottom of the social hierarchy.[4] From the time when it became customary to pass names down from one generation to another, naming became an element in the system of kinship.[5] However, parents, or whoever else was responsible for choosing a child's name, remained able to make a free choice, for they could take a name from outside the kingroup, favor one side of the family or the other, or associate their child by name with another kingroup (*Ansippung*). Their choice would have been influenced by a range of factors, political, religious, or economic.[6] In my analysis of inherited names, I shall start by asking what patterns of naming suggest about the system of kinship, and whether this image of kinship conforms with what we already know about kinship and other social groupings. Then in the second part of my paper I shall examine how the custom of naming changed, for within the period characterized by the use of a single name, there was nevertheless a shift from the transmission of names by means of variation (the inheritance of name elements) to transmission by means of repetition (the inheritance of an entire name). I shall ask whether

---

[4]For Bavaria, see Ludwig Holzfurtner, "Untersuchungen zur Namengebung im frühen Mittelalter nach der bayerischen Quellen des achten und neunten Jahrhunderts," *Zeitschrift für die bayerische Landesgeschichte* 45 (1982), 3–21. For Swabia, see Hans-Werner Goetz, "Zur Namengebung in der alamanischen Grundbesitzerschicht der Karolingerzeit. Ein Beitrag zur Familienforschung," *Zeitschrift für die Geschichte des Oberrheins* 133 (1985), 1–41. For *Francia*, land of the Franks, see Le Jan, *Famille et pouvoir*, pp. 180–82.

[5]Hans-Walter Klewitz, "Namengebung und Sippenbewußtsein in den deutschen Königs-familien des 10.–12. Jahrhunderts," *Archiv für Urkundenforschung* 18 (1944), 23–37. Karl Schmid, "Zur Problematik von Familie, Sippe und Geschlecht. Haus und Dynastie beim milttelalterlichen Adel," *Zeitschrift für die Geschichte des Oberrheins* 105 (1957), 1–62. Wilhelm Störmer, *Früher Adel. Studien zur politischen Führungsschicht im fränkisch-deutschen Reich vom 8. bis 11. Jahrhundert* (Stuttgart, 1973), 2:29–55. Karl-Ferdinand Werner, "Liens de parenté et noms de personne. Un problème historique et méthodol-ogique," in Georges Duby and Jacques Le Goff, eds., *Famille et parenté dans l'Occident médiéval: Actes du Colloque de Paris (6–8 Juin 1974)*, (Paris, 1977), pp. 13–18.

[6]Le Jan, *Famille et pouvoir*, pp. 188–92.

this important shift was the result of changes in the system of kinship or whether it has to be explained by reference to other cultural phenomena.

In addressing the first question, we must begin by establishing from which side of the family names were chosen. We can state immediately that the system of name-giving was bilateral: first of all, name elements and then entire names crossed back and forth between the male and female sides of a family, for names originating in the paternal line might be given to daughters, and names from the maternal line might be used for sons. In the sixth and seventh centuries, an ancient custom consisted of mixing paternal and maternal name elements, thus:

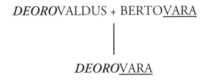

The root of the name *Deorovara, Deoro,* came from her father, and the suffix, *-vara,* from her mother.[7] Although this practice died out in the course of the seventh century, the transmission of elements or of entire names continued to draw from both sides of the family. Several examples are: *Uulf-gunda,* daughter of Uulf-oald (seventh century), Hugh the Abbot, son of Conrad and Adalheid, named after his maternal grandfather (mid-ninth century), Gisela, daughter of Eberhard of Friouli and Gisela (mid-ninth century), and Robert, son of Count Megingald, named after his maternal grandfather (end of the ninth century).

This system corresponds with the early medieval kinship system which we know to have been bilateral. Membership in the kingroup and the rights that went with it were transmitted through both the paternal and the maternal lines. The kingroup *parentela,* as defined in the law codes and recognized by legal systems and the groups of kinfolk that assured

---

[7]Hartmut Atsma and Jean Vezin, eds., *Chartae latinae antiquiores* 592 (Zurich, 1981).

social stability, had a completely cognatic structure.[8] In addition, the rules of marriage established the woman as the keystone of alliances between kingroups and also as the channel for the transmission of rights. In principle, the married woman preserved her own property and administered it as she wished. Finally, residence was virilocal, which is characteristic of bilateral kinship systems.[9]

However, further examination of patterns of naming reveals that within this bilaterality there were strong patrilinear tendencies. Hans-Werner Goetz has conducted painstaking studies on names in Swabia in the eighth and ninth centuries that have shown that name-giving was more commonly agnatic than cognatic.[10] Using charters from Werden in Saxony, Saint-Gall in Alemannia, and the polyptych of Saint-Germain-des-Prés, he has also compared the naming of women in three different parts of the Carolingian empire. This study has shown that at all social levels throughout the Carolingian period, children were more frequently named after their fathers than after their mothers.[11] I have myself demonstrated that in the area between the Rhine and the Loire in the eighth and ninth centuries, 50 percent of children were named for the paternal side of their family and only 16 percent for the maternal side.[12] Habits of name-giving were therefore not gender-neutral, for the paternal and maternal lines were not of equal significance. Naming patterns thus suggest an image of kinship that was cognatic, but nevertheless had a strong patrilinear emphasis. Similarly, if we shift a moment to consider the ways in

---

[8]Le Jan, *Famille et pouvoir*, pp. 225–50, and "Nommer/identifier ou la puissance du nom dans la société du haut Moyen Age," in *Des noms et des Hommes. Sources Travaux Historiques* 45/46 (1996), 47–56. Proceedings of the Table Ronde, organized by *Histoire au Present*.

[9]Le Jan, *Famille et pouvoir*, pp. 334–38.

[10]Goetz, "Zur Namengebung," pp. 1–41.

[11]Hans-Werner Goetz, "Nomen Feminile. Namen und Namengebung der Frauen im frühen Mittelalter," *Francia* 23/1 (1996), 99–127.

[12]Le Jan, *Famille et pouvoir*, pp. 185–87.

which families functioned, it is evident that men and women did not in fact enjoy the same rights, functions, and powers. The advantage lay with the men. In matters of inheritance, sons were preferred over daughters.

Until the tenth century, marriage alliances were made with women of the same social status, and rarely with women of higher status. Political and economic authority were exercised by men. Even if the house was a woman's privileged space, under her own administration, a wife only exercised a delegated authority there, for she remained under the protection of her husband and her property was integrated into the household property and administered by her husband.[13] Name-giving thus not only reflected the rules of kinship, it was also adapted to social realities and familial strategies.

We can take this analysis further by examining the way in which names from the paternal and the maternal lines were used within individual families. I shall use the example of the family of Eberhard of Friuli and his wife Gisela, daughter of Louis the Pious and Judith (see next page).[14]

Eberhard and Judith had nine children, five sons and four daughters. Five children were named for the paternal line, and four for the maternal side, a more or less even ratio. However, of the five paternal names, four were given to sons, and the fifth to the eldest daughter who was named for her paternal grandmother. Only the fifth son was named after a relative on his mother's side (her own mother's uncle). Part of the explanation for this pattern may be that Gisela was unable to transmit to her sons the male royal names of the Carolingians carried by her father and brothers (*Louis, Lothar, Pippin* and *Charles*).

In the tenth and eleventh centuries, naming patterns changed as aristocratic lineages developed around the patrilinear inheritance of *honores*,

---

[13] Le Jan, *Famille et pouvoir*, pp. 351–54. Also see Le Jan, "L'épouse du comte au IXe siècle. Evolution d'un modèle et idéologie du pouvoir," in *Femmes et pouvoirs des femmes dans le haut Moyen Age et à Byzance*, ed. Stephane Lebecq, Régine Le Jan, Alain Dierkens, and Jean-Marie Sansterre (Lille, 1999), 65–73.

[14] *Cartulaire de l'abbaye de Cysoing*, ed. Ignace de Coussemaker, 1 (Lille, 1883), 8.

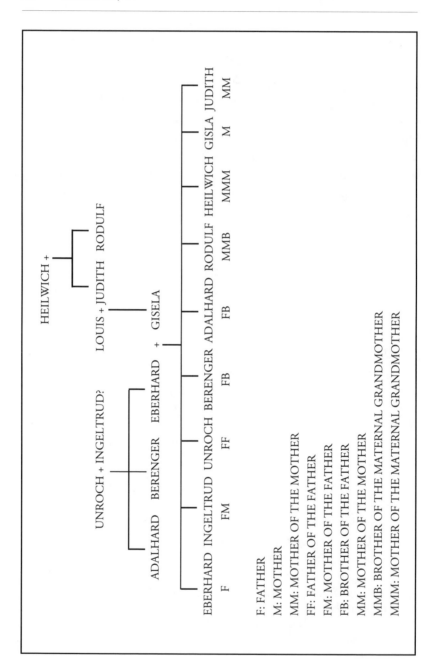

F: FATHER
M: MOTHER
MM: MOTHER OF THE MOTHER
FF: FATHER OF THE FATHER
FM: MOTHER OF THE FATHER
FB: BROTHER OF THE FATHER
MM: MOTHER OF THE MOTHER
MMB: BROTHER OF THE MATERNAL GRANDMOTHER
MMM: MOTHER OF THE MATERNAL GRANDMOTHER

and as the enforcement of the rules of marriage took effect. The shift in naming patterns was not a shift toward patrilinearity so much as toward a greater emphasis on hierarchy. We can trace the emergence of male leading names (*Stammname*), which were given to one or two sons likely to inherit, but which might also be transmitted via daughters. Names from the mother's family continued to be used and to cross from one lineage into another as marriage alliances were made and as parental choice was exercised.

The table on the next page shows how the names characteristic of the "Robertian" family, *Odo, Hugh* and *Emma*, passed into the name stock of the "Theobaldian" family, via the marriage of King Robert's granddaughter Liutgard to Theobald the Trickster, count of Blois and Chartres.[15]

Within the naming patterns of these aristocratic lineages, use of names from the mother's family seems to have increased. This corresponds to a redefinition of the role of the wife and of the female line within family structures. As a result of the combined effects of the patrimonialization of power, together with the practice of marrying higher-status wives and an emphasis on the conjugal family, a wife's rights were defined and her primary role in transmitting nobility was affirmed.[16] These brief comments confirm that naming is a complex social phenomenon, and that name-

---

[15]For other examples, see Le Jan, *Famille et pouvoir*, pp. 214–22. Also see Christian Settipani, "Les comtes d'Anjou et leurs alliances aux Xe et XIe siècles," in *Family Trees and the Roots of Politics. The Prosopography of Britain and France from the Tenth to the Twelfth Century*, ed. K. S. B. Keats-Rohan (Woodbridge, Suffolk, 1997), pp. 265–66.

[16]In this regard, see the speech of Adalberon of Laon against the election of Charles of Lower Lotharingia as King of France in 987. He invokes the humble origins of Charles's wife, *"uxor de militari ordine."* The speech was doubtless never given and the reasoning could well have been reversed. Still, it shows that at a conceptual level the matrimonial system was henceforth isogamic and that the spouse of a *princeps* should come from an illustrious princely, and even royal, family, in that her nobility reflected on her husband, either weakening or strengthening it. Sigebert de Gembloux writes, "Hildebrand distinguished himself among the nobles of Brabant through his family, his wealth, and by the fact that his nobility was increased through another nobility, for he had married Renuidis, daughter of our very noble lord Wicbert" (Sigebert de Gembloux, *Vita Wicberti* 18, MGH SS 8:513).

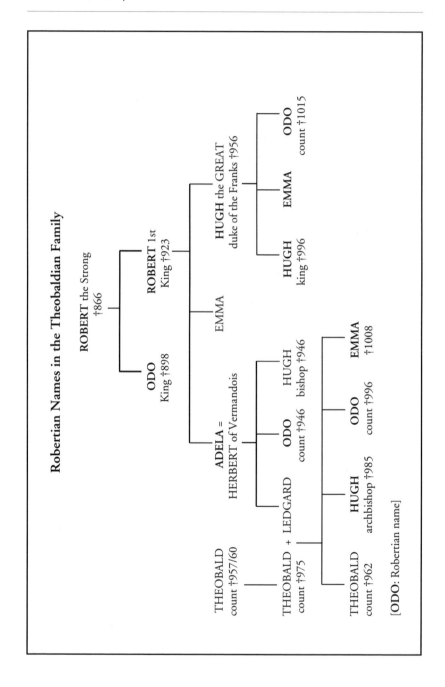

Robertian Names in the Theobaldian Family

ROBERT the Strong †866

ROBERT 1st King †923

ODO King †898

HUGH the GREAT duke of the Franks †956

EMMA

HUGH king †996

EMMA

ODO count †1015

ADELA = HERBERT of Vermandois

HUGH bishop †946

ODO count †946

THEOBALD count †957/60

THEOBALD + LEDGARD count †975

HUGH archbishop †985

ODO count †996

EMMA †1008

THEOBALD count †962

[ODO: Robertian name]

giving customs evolved within kinship systems, changing as the structure, organization, and inheritance strategies of families changed.

To turn now to my second theme: was the switch from naming by element variation to the repetition of whole names (*Nachbennenung*) associated with the changing structure of kinship, or must we seek other explanations?

The Romans were familiar with the principle of variation, but it remained little used until the end of antiquity.[17] Instead, the Romans made very heavy use of naming repetition. This was closely associated with the cult of ancestors, originally in the context of the patrilinear gens, and later within increasingly bilateral contexts.[18] The Germanic peoples, on the other hand, had no domestic cult of ancestors, and named their offspring according to the principle of variation, transmitting the two elements of each name separately. As Michael Mitterauer has shown, there was also a religious aspect to early Germanic naming practices.[19] Composed of the two elements, a Germanic name had a strong totemic quality.[20] German historians, notably Wolfgang Haubrich, Dieter Geuenich and Hans-Werner Goetz, have demonstrated the importance of the *nomen* as both symbol and meaning (*signum* and *significatio*). It expressed the nature of an individual, his essence.[21] Germanic belief in the corporeal and spiritual

---

[17]Martin Heinzelmann, "Les changements de la dénomination latine à la fin de l'Antiquité," in *Famille et parenté*, ed. Duby and Le Goff, p. 23.

[18]*Famille et parenté*, ed. Duby and Le Goff, p. 21, and Mitterauer, *Ahnen und Heilige*, pp. 78–82.

[19]Mitterauer, *Ahnen und Heilige*, pp. 223–40.

[20]This aspect has been well highlighted by Störmer for Bavaria, in *Früher Adel*, p. 4. See also Ermold le Noir explaining the meaning of the name of Louis and the glorious future for which that name had destined him since birth, in *Poème sur Louis le Pieux et Épîtres au roi Pépin*, ed. and trans. Edmond Faral (Paris, 1964), p. 11.

[21]Goetz, "Nomen feminile," pp. 100–01, and "Nomen. Zur Bedeutung von Personennamen in der frühmittelalterlichen Gesellschaft," *Onomastik: Akten des 18. Internationalen Kongresses für Namenforschung* (1999).

integrity of the dead person, in effect in the survival of an individual after death, made it impossible to hand on the *nomen* of that person. But the constituent elements of that *nomen* could be inherited if they were deemed to belong to the gens as a whole. Naming by varying the elements thus allowed a name to retain all its power to identify someone as a member of a kingroup without violating the taboo attached to the *nomen*. In effect, the principle of variation maintained familial identity without thereby maintaining the memory of ancestors.[22]

The transmission of entire names began in the fifth century in the Burgundian ruling family,[23] followed shortly by the Merovingian dynasty. The earliest examples of name repetition (*Nachbennenung*) among the Merovingians are associated with strategies of artificial kinship (*Ansippung*). At virtually the same moment Chlodomer of Orléans and Chlothar I of Soissons each named a son *Gunthar* (the second son of Chlodomer, born around 517–24, and the first son of Chlothar, born circa 517–18), the name of an earlier Burgundian king.[24] The political aspect of this is obvious: artificial kinship allowed the Merovingians to attach themselves to the Burgundian dynasty and thus to present themselves as legitimate heirs to the Burgundian kings whom they were seeking to eliminate.[25] This artificial kinship inaugurated the use of name repetition among the Merovingians. Chlothar I named his second son (born circa 519) after his grandfather Childeric, thereby stressing the link between the Salian Franks and their territorial heritage.[26] Chlothar subsequently named one of his sons *Sigebert*, a name borne by the king of the Rhineland Franks, Sigebert

---

[22]Le Jan, *Famille et pouvoir*, pp. 52–54 and 193–200, and "Nommer/identifier," pp. 49–50.

[23]Mitterauer, *Ahnen und Heilige*, p. 233.

[24]Mitterauer, *Ahnen und Heilige*, p. 233 and Eugen Ewig, "Die Namengebung bei den ältesten Frankenkönigen und im merowingischen Königshaus," *Francia* 19 (1991), 41.

[25]Ewig, "Die Namengebung," p. 42.

[26]Ewig, "Die Namengebung," p. 29.

the Lame. As far as daughters are concerned, the first attested examples of name repetition date from the generation of Chlothar I's grandchildren (Basina, daughter of Chilperic I, born circa 555–65; Chrodichild, daughter of Charibert I, born about 560–65; Ingund, daughter of Sigebert, born about 567).[27]

Naming by repetition was not restricted to royal families, precociously organized into lineages. At the end of the sixth century, Bishop Bertramn of Le Mans, born about 540, bore the name of his maternal uncle, the bishop of Bordeaux. One of his great-nephews, Leutramnus, had the name of his maternal grandfather.[28] In the seventh century, repetition spread to Austria; a granddaughter of Duke Gunduin received the name of her grandmother on her mother's side, *Saretrudis*, and another of his granddaughters was called after her paternal grandmother, *Aba*.[29] Pippin II, who was probably born shortly after 640, was named after his maternal grandfather, and the examples could be continued. The custom spread very widely in the eighth and ninth centuries, and by the tenth century was in use throughout Frankish society.[30]

Although its use remained limited for a long time, the transmission of entire names was an important innovation in Romanic-Germanic cultures, for it was associated with Christianization.[31] In Roman society the *nomen* had no taboos associated with it, and by transmitting the names

---

[27]Ewig, "Die Namengebung," pp. 38–39.

[28]Margarete Weidemann, *Das Testament des Bischofs Berthramn von Le Mans vom 27. März 616. Untersuchungen zur Besitz und Geschichte einer fränkischer [fränkischen?] Familie im 6. und 7. Jahrhundert* (Mainz, 1986), and U. Nonn, "Eine fränkische Adelssippe um 600. Zur Familie des Bischofs Berthram von Le Mans," *Frühmittelalterliche Studien* 9 (1975), 188–201.

[29]*Vita Sadalbergae abbatissae Laudunensis*, MGH SSRM 5:55.

[30]Le Jan, *Famille et pouvoir*, pp. 206–14, and "Entre maîtres et dépendants: Réflexions sur la famille paysanne en Lotharingie, aux IXe et Xe siècles," in *Campagnes médiévales. L'homme et son espace. Etudes offertes à Robert Fossier* (Paris, 1995), pp. 280–83.

[31]Mitterauer, *Ahnen und Heilige*, p. 230.

of parents (whether natal or adoptive) and of uncles and aunts, naming created a link that helped to maintain the cult of ancestors.[32] But Christian bishops reacted against the cult of ancestors with its pagan associations, and some, such as John Chrysostom in the fourth century, spoke out against the habit of giving ancestral names to a child. In spite of this, Christian families continued to pass on the names of close relatives to their children, even though Christianization had had a great impact on the choice of names used in late antiquity. The inheritance of an entire name was thus not intrinsically Christian, but in the late Roman world it was particularly associated with the Christian communities of the empire.[33] Christianization thus broke the taboo surrounding the *nomen* in Germanic culture and, starting with royal dynasties, allowed the adoption of name repetition.[34] Nevertheless, in the sixth century, the Merovingians transmitted only the names of relatives who were already dead, as though the taboo associated with the *nomen* still clung to the living.[35] It was the same with the various Anglo-Saxon ruling families of the seventh and eighth centuries. Among the Frankish aristocracy of the seventh century, the names of parents were never given to children, any more than were the names of uncles and aunts. The entire name thus associated an individual with one of his or her deceased ancestors.[36] Only in the eighth century did the

---

[32]Mitterauer, *Ahnen und Heilige*, pp. 79–80.

[33]Mitterauer, *Ahnen und Heilige*, p. 86.

[34]Mitterauer, *Ahnen und Heilige*, p. 230.

[35]Michael Mitterauer, "Zur Nachbenennung nach Lebenden und Toten in Fürstenhäusern des Frühmittelalters," in *Gesellschaftsgeschichte. Festschrift für Karl Bosl zum 80. geburtstag*, 2 vols. (Munich, 1988), 1:386–99. In the seventh century Clotaire, son of Theodebert II, who was born ca. 610–11, received the same name as a son of Chilperic who died around 629. Dagobert, son of Childeric II and Bilechild, received the name of his maternal uncle, Dagobert II, during the latter's lifetime. In both cases the political circumstances were unusual.

[36]Karl August Eckhardt, *Irdische Unsterblichkeit. Germanischer Glaube an die Wiederverkörperung in der Sippe* (Weimar, 1937).

names of living relatives begin to be handed down, doubtless in response to increasing Christianization.

Apart from the Merovingians, who abandoned variation in naming their sons after 565[37] despite continuing to use it for their daughters into the seventh century,[38] naming by repetition (*Nachbennenung*) long remained a rare practice. Variation remained the standard practice among the Frankish aristocracy until the end of the eighth century, and among the rest of the Frankish population until the tenth century. For several centuries, variation and repetition were thus in use simultaneously, often within the same families.[39] Among the Anglo-Saxons, variation remained in use even longer, for repetition did not even begin to be used until the very end of the tenth century.

There were probably several reasons for the co-existence of variation and repetition. They reflected different forms of kin relationships: variation integrated the individual into the kingroup and defined membership of the familial group who shared a stock of name elements, while repetition stressed one-on-one links. Naming by variation reflected the overlapping circles of kinship around an individual, and was well adapted to broad, bilateral kingroups.[40] Proceeding outwards from the basic unit of descent, the nuclear family, it emphasized the cohesion of the sibling group through the use of the same final element.[41]

---

[37]Ewig, "Die Namengebung," p. 27.

[38]Ewig, "Die Namengebung," pp. 38–39.

[39]Le Jan, *Famille et pouvoir*, pp. 208–14.

[40]Le Jan, *Famille et pouvoir*, pp. 193–200.

[41]Sources for Table 1: *Regesta Alsatiae aevi Merovingi et Karolini (496–918)*, ed. Albert Brückner, 1 (Strasburg, 1949), pp. 113, 126, 133, 134, 135, 145, 147, and 154. Sources for Table 2: *Urkundenbuch zur Geschichte der mittelrheinishen Territorien*, ed. Heinrich Beyer, Leopold Eltester, and Adam Goerz, 1 (Koblenz, 1860), p. 25; Karl Glöckner, ed., *Codex Laureshamensis*, 3 vols. (Darmstadt, 1929), 1:415, 487, 528, 710, 713, 760, and 2291.

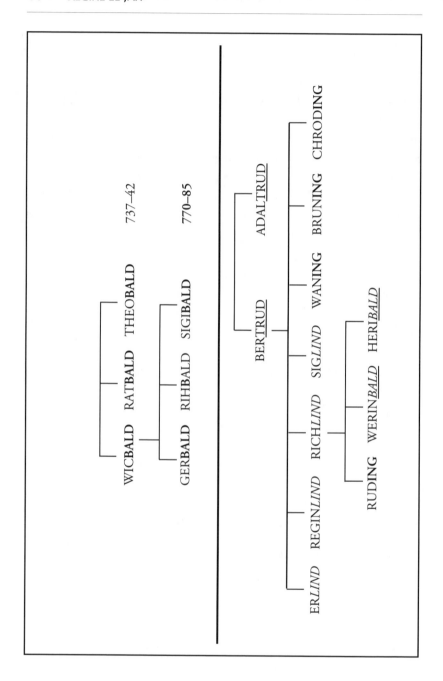

A group of siblings would also be situated within a large horizontal group of cousins, identifiable by common name elements that functioned as signs recognizable to all the members of the same *Sippe*. The integrative function of naming by variation was suited to the early medieval *Sippen*: large, bilateral, horizontally-structured kingroups held together by criss-crossing marital alliances renewed over several generations and supported by local solidarities and interspersed inheritance and jurisdictions (*potestates*).

By contrast, naming by repetition created or reinforced specific ties between one person and an ancestor, relative, or saint. It also emphasized the ideological aspect of a name. The Merovingian predilection for the name of their eponymous ancestor, Merovech, and for the name of his son, Childeric (also the name of the very last Merovingian king), obviously contributed to building a dynasty.[42] We can easily understand why repetition served the interests and ambitions of royal families, both because of the opportunity for claims of artificial kinship (*Ansippung*) and because a link was rapidly established between a royal name and the capacity to rule. This is particularly evident among the Carolingians. From Charlemagne onward, only legitimate sons carried a royal name (*Charles, Louis, Lothar, Pippin*) while the others carried non-royal Carolingian names, notably *Drogo, Arnulf,* or *Bernard,*[43] or names from their maternal side. Daughters either had Carolingian names such as *Gisela* or the names of Carolingian queens, particularly *Hildegard, Ermengard, Judith,* and *Ermentrude,* but they were unable to transmit the royal names to their sons. The exceptions to this occur only in the context of the politics of the last years of the ninth century and the early tenth century, and they thereby confirm the fundamental link between name and royal power. The most significant

---

[42]Ewig, "Die Namengebung," pp. 31–33.

[43]On the illegitimacy of Bernard of Italy, son of Pepin of Italy, see Johannes Fried, "Elite und Ideologie oder die Nachfolgeordnung Karls des Grossens vom Jahre 813," in *La royauté et les élites dans l'Europe carolingienne (du début du IXe aux environs de 920)*, ed. Régine Le Jan (Lille, 1998), pp. 90–109.

such exception is the son of Boso of Provence and his wife Ermengard, daughter of Louis II. Born in 880, after his father's election as king of Burgundy and Provence, the child was named *Louis* after his maternal grandfather. The choice of name was a means of legitimizing both his father's power and his own right to succeed.[44] In aristocratic families in the tenth and eleventh centuries, names served to underline claims to this or that inheritance,[45] and the clerical names that emerged during the barbarian period[46] reflect this same ideological aspect of naming.[47]

By handing down entire names, families added a personal, vertically-oriented and programmatic dimension to a system of naming that continued to stress the group and its integration into a large kindred like the

[44]Le Jan, *Famille et pouvoir*, p. 205. Stuart Airlie, "Semper fideles? Loyauté envers les Carolingiens comme constituant de l'identité aristocratiquée," in *La royauté*, ed. Le Jan, p. 140.

[45]After the end of the ninth century, the ties between name and honor become clearer. In Metz in 861 there was a count Liutard. Between 872 and 889–90 the count was Adalhard, son of the senechal of the same name who was himself father of a Liutard. The senechal had lived in Lotharingian between 844 and 860–61, and his son had married there. In 907–09 there was another Liutard and then a son of Adalhard (see Eduard Hlawitschka, "Die altere Matfredingen und die Adalharde im 9. Jhr," in *Die Anfänge des Hauses Habsburg-Lothringen. Genealogische Untersuchungen zur Geschichte Lothringens und des Reiches im 9., 10. und 11. Jahrhundert* [Sarrebrück, 1969], pp. 154–71). In the family naming system, the clan names given to eldest sons destined them to inherit the family honor. Nonetheless there was no absolute rule linking name and honor. Younger sons could inherit if the eldest died, and the same held true for daughters when there were no sons. The latter passed their inheritance to their sons without them being necessarily named after their mother's family. The naming system was thus more complex than that of inheritance.

[46]Dietrich Claude, *Adel, Kirche und Königtum im Westgotenreich* (Sigmaringen, 1971), p. 108.

[47]The son of Adele of Anjou and of Gautier of Amiens was named *Gui*, like his maternal uncle, and like the latter he was bishop of Amiens (doubtless after 976). In the comital family of Anjou, *Gui* was a clerical name: Gui, priest of Saint-Martin of Tours in 914, Gui, canon of Saint-Martin of Tours then bishop of Soissons, his nephews Gui, bishop of le Puy and Gui, bishop of Soissons. *Adalberon* had a similar role in the family of Ardenne in the tenth and eleventh centuries.

Sippe. When naming by variation was finally abandoned and repetition became the exclusive practice, there was a complete change of perspective as the emphasis now lay with the individual person and the kingroup retreated into the background. What was the cause of this change? In the first place, it certainly involved the changing self-images of society, family, and kinship. In the Carolingian period, the Church succeeded in imposing the patristic vision of a patriarchal society arrayed in order under the authority of king and father. The Church promulgated the notion that, other than the nuclear family, the only family which counted for anything in God's eyes was the family of all baptized people, all sons of God and brothers in Christ. The Carolingian Church also imposed the model of the conjugal Christian family.[48] We are certainly now talking about ideology rather than social practice, but Christian ideology was obviously an important factor in the transmission of the names of living relatives and the abandonment of variation.

Changes in naming patterns also reflected social practice and the growing emphasis on hierarchically-ordered kingroups. Families continued to using naming strategies to associate a group of siblings with their cognatic kin, and they continued to choose names from a narrow genealogical pool restricted to the third degree, the limit of effective kinship. Naming by repetition no longer outlined the fluid contours of a *Sippe,* but instead marked out precise, carefully selected lines.[49]

Over two generations, the names handed down within the family of the counts of Flanders attached that family to four groups: the Carolingians, via the names *Arnulf, Hildegard,* and *Ermentrude;* the West Saxon dynasty via the names *Æthelwulf* (Adalulf), *Ealswith* (Ealswide), and *Egbert;* the counts of Vermandois via the name *Liutgard* (sister of Adela of

---

[48]Pierre Toubert, "La théorie du mariage chez les moralistes carolingiens," *Il Matrimonio nella società altomedievale* 24 (1977), 233–82, and "L'institution du mariage chrétien, de l'Antiquité tardive à l'an mil," *Morfologie sociali e culturali in Europa fra tarda antichità e alto medioevo* 45 (1998), 503–53.

[49]Le Jan, *Famille et pouvoir,* p. 218.

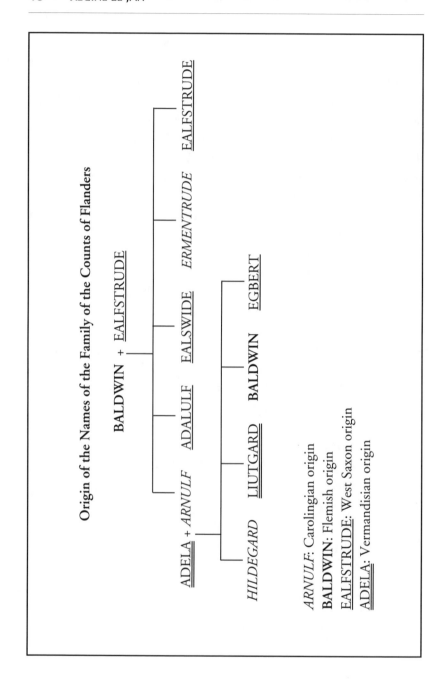

Origin of the Names of the Family of the Counts of Flanders

BALDWIN + <u>EALFSTRUDE</u>

ADELA + *ARNULF*   <u>ADALULF</u>   <u>EALSWIDE</u>   *ERMENTRUDE*   EALFSTRUDE

HILDEGARD   <u>LIUTGARD</u>   **BALDWIN**   <u>EGBERT</u>

ARNULF: Carolingian origin
BALDWIN: Flemish origin
<u>EALFSTRUDE</u>: West Saxon origin
<u>ADELA</u>: Vermandisian origin

Vermandois); and finally, the strictly Flemish group, via *Baldwin*. Each name belonged to a specific lineage, and together they underlined the illustriousness of a family and the importance of its network of relatives. One measure of tenth-century Ottonian power is the diffusion of Ottonian names into others' families.[50]

It is now time to conclude. Naming patterns in the early Middle Ages were particularly complex because each person had only one name. That name had to designate the individual, express both personal and family characteristics, integrate its bearer into the kingroup, and represent him or her to the wider world. In general, name-giving was cognatic, exactly like the system of kinship with which it was associated. But it was also adaptable to the ways in which families functioned in practice and to social conventions. Finally, it reflected society's self-image and its use of symbolism. The use of names to create artificial claims to kinship (*Ansippung*) reveals the symbolic aspect; the adoption of naming by repetition (*Nachbennenung*) hints at changing notions of the sacred; and the abandonment of naming by the variation of elements is a witness to the image of the conjugal family that a Christianized society constructed for itself, reflecting also the growing emphasis on hierarchically-ordered kingroups.

---

[50]Le Jan, *Famille et pouvoir*, p. 221.

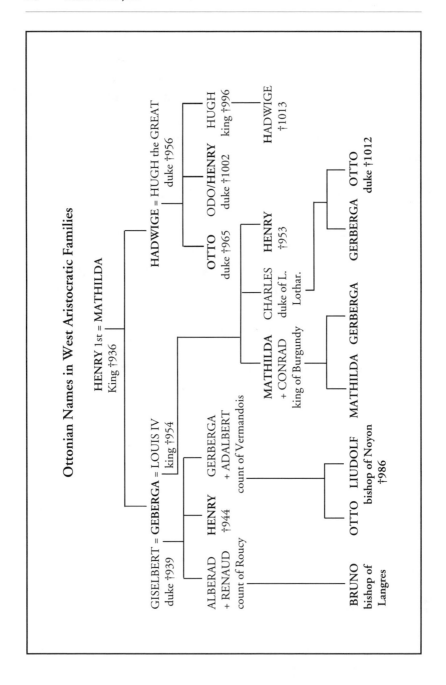

Ottonian Names in West Aristocratic Families

Part III

Personal Names in Southern Europe (Tenth to Thirteenth Centuries)

Personal Naming and Structures of Kinship in the Medieval Spanish Peasantry

Lluís To Figueras

The evolution of personal naming in the northern Iberian Peninsula between the ninth and thirteenth centuries has recently been analyzed in a collective overview from a comparative perspective using the same methods applied to other regions. In this paper I will try to summarize the evidence dealing with the evolution of names as a clue for the interpretation of the structures of kinship among peasantry.[1]

Sharing Names in the High Middle Ages

As was true nearly everywhere in western Europe, the single name was a dominant pattern in most of the northern Spanish kingdoms and counties during the ninth and tenth centuries. Galicia, Bierzo, and Liébana in the northwest and Catalonia in the northeast are among the European regions in which more than 80 percent and perhaps as many as 90 percent of the individuals encountered are referred to by a single name or a name with a complementary element or functional adjunct, such as king, count, or priest. There is an important exception in the kingdom of Navarre, including the region of Rioja, conquered by the kings of Pamplona at the beginning of the tenth century, and to some extent the neighboring areas of Castile and Aragón, as will be examined later.

Related to this model of a single name pattern is the huge stock of different names used by people out of the need to avoid confusion, a

---

[1]*Antroponimia y sociedad. Sistemas de identificación hispano-cristianos en los siglos IX a XIII,* ed. Pascual Martínez Sopena (Santiago de Compostela-Valladolid, 1995).

situation that exists nearly everywhere in the tenth century. This stock of names was extremely large but not unlimited.

If we take into account lists of people from a single community, we will always find a small number of homonyms. One hundred and four individuals of the Catalan village of Artés bore 85 different names in 938 and 251 men from some villages near St. Joan de les Abadesses used 180 different names in 913. But some of these names were duplicated in both places. For example, 28 of the 85 names in the first village can be found among the list from St. Joan de les Abadesses. In a third list of 96 men from another Catalan village, Vilamacolum, in 916, there are also homonyms within the community and in relation to the others. Ten of the names could be found at the same time in these three different communities, which were quite far from each other: *Agila, Eldefredo, Franco, Galindo, Iohannes, Miro, Recosindo, Sunegildes, Traserico,* and *Vincemalo.*[2]

Obviously, the larger the sample is, the greater the chances are of finding repetition. Thus in Catalonia the total of 39,159 people figuring in charters prior to 1000 bore a total of 4,176 different names! More than half of these occurred only once.[3]

In this context it is difficult to say whether a name is common or rare. This is due to the fact that a name could be rare in a single peasant community but, as in the cases above, it could be borne by people living in different communities and also by people living simultaneously in far-flung regions. A female name like *Ailo* could be found in Catalonia and in Liébana in the tenth century. The same holds true for *Froila,* found in León and in Catalonia, and others as well.

This means that these regions in the north of Spain were to some extent sharing similar cultural traditions, and that there were no closed cultural boundaries between Spain and the south of France. A common

---

[2]Lluís To Figueras, "Antroponimia de los condados catalanes (Barcelona, Girona y Osona, siglos X–XII)," in *Antroponimia y sociedad,* ed. Martínez Sopena, pp. 371–94.

[3]Jordi Bolòs i Masclans and Josep Moran i Ocerinjauregui, *Repertori d'Antropònims catalans* 1 (Barcelona, 1994). But some of these 4,176 names could be considered variations of the same one, as in *Aldericus* and *Eldericus.*

background could, for example, have been related to the Latin or Visigothic past, and it is well known how close northern Spain was during the
tenth century to some features of the Visigothic heritage, especially in the
kingdom of Asturias, which considered itself to be an heir to the kingdom
of Toledo. In Catalonia, on the other hand, Visigothic culture emphasized
its distinctiveness within the Carolingian Empire.[4]

On the other hand, some names could be characteristic of a single
region where the prestige of a local saint served to popularize his name
among the people.[5] Each region could have its own specific stock of names
with elements in common with neighboring regions, and measuring the
disparities between different stocks of names will therefore always be prob-
lematic. Thus, attempts to represent differences in name stocks on a map
are highly questionable.

In any case, by the tenth century names were not a mark of ethnic
identity. Having a Germanic name did not automatically prove Germanic
ancestry. We can easily find out that brothers of the same family bore both
Germanic and Christian names, and despite the large number of people
using Germanic names there is no archeological proof that this stems from
an important settlement of Visigothic peoples in the north of Spain. It is
perfectly possible to explain such diversity in terms of varying cultural
influences acting on the same community. Of course this is not the case
for the Jews and Muslims, or for immigrant populations like the *mozárabes*
or the *francos* living in the cities. All of them offer good examples of how
names could be a clear mark of social identity.[6]

---

[4]Michel Zimmermann, "Aux origines de la Catalogne. Géographie politique et affirmation
nationale," *Le Moyen Age* 89 (1983), 5–40; and Jacques Fontaine and Christine Pellistrandi, eds., *L'Europe héritière de l'Espagne wisigothique* (Madrid, 1992).

[5]See the examples of *Justa* and *Isidoro* in León in Pascual Martínez Sopena, "La antroponímia leonesa. Un estudio del Archivo Catedral de León (876–1200)," in *Antroponimia
y sociedad*, ed. Martínez Sopena, pp. 155–80.

[6]Carlos Laliena Corbera, "La antroponímia de los mudéjares: resistencia y aculturación de
una minoría," in *L'anthroponymie. Document de l'histoire sociale des mondes méditerranéens
médiévaux*, ed. Monique Bourin, Jean-Marie Martin, and François Menant (Rome, 1996),

There is also no evidence that single names were a useful social indicator during this period. There were not any names reserved specifically for peasants or aristocrats. On the contrary, in the lists from peasant communities we find names used by counts or kings. For example the name *Pelayo*, as well known as any in use at the time, is shared by individuals of very different social categories. Nevertheless, among noblemen, names were an important way of showing ancestral descent, as has been proved for the Carolingian world.[7]

Even over distances in space and in time, bearing a particular name could be seen as making a claim on collective rights and domains, political influence, or religious prestige of a given family. But at the peasant level two persons having the same name does not indicate that they were related by kinship, especially when they lived in distant villages. Inside a single community, homonyms could appear just because people were sharing the same stock of names, and in this context, even if children received their names from their ancestors, parents, uncles, or more distant kin, we can doubt that names were useful for showing a parental link.

Single Names and Kinship

The use of single names is a custom that is consistent with what we know about family structure. During the tenth century most peasants were living in village communities as freemen, and in households that were mainly conjugal units with children. Agrarian property was possessed by individuals or household units that rarely extended beyond the married couple and its children. But frequently what gave the right to hold land and to plough uncultivated land was membership in a community. The

pp. 143–66; and Juan Ignacio Ruiz de la Peña Solar, "La antroponimia como indicador de fenómenos de movilidad geográfica: el ejemplo de las colonizaciones francas en el Oviedo medieval (1100–1230)," in *Antroponimia y sociedad*, ed. Martínez Sopena , pp. 133–54.

[7]Régine Le Jan, *Famille et pouvoir dans le monde franc (VIIe–Xe siècle). Essai d'anthropologie sociale* (Paris, 1995), pp. 179–223.

access to certain elements of the territory surrounding the village was reserved for all members of the peasant community. The first appearances of communitarian institutions (*concilium*) were probably related to these collective concerns.[8]

There is no contradiction between family and community membership and the access to community rights and duties was probably made through the family household units. Nevertheless, in many regions peasants could obtain land outside the rules of inheritance because there were still lands available, and also because there were institutions and a social context that favored the taking of new lands by the peasants (*aprisio, pressura, escalio*).[9] Also, lords could provide lands to new couples wishing to establish themselves away from their parents' homes. In a well-known example from the kingdom of León, a village was first occupied by a single family that in the next generation appeared to divide into several household units at the same time that other settlers were arriving to join the village community. Many other villages undoubtedly developed in the same way during these years. Partible inheritance was the rule with the consequence that in every generation family farms were rearranged.[10]

Names bearing no indication of filiation were used at this time in a context in which inheritance was not the only way to obtain land and in

---

[8]José Ángel García de Cortázar, "Les communautés villageoises du nord de la Péninsule ibérique au Moyen Age," in *Les communautés villageoises en Europe occidentale, du Moyen Age aux temps modernes* (Auch, France, 1984), pp. 55–77; Pierre Bonnassie and Pierre Guichard, "Les communautés rurales en Catalogne et dans le Pays Valencien (IXe–milieu XIVe siècle)," ibid., pp. 79–115.

[9]After the classic works of Claudio Sánchez Albornoz see also: Pierre Bonnassie, "Du Rhone à la Galice: genèse et modalités du régime féodal," in *Structures féodales et féodalisme dans l'Occident méditerranéen* (Rome, 1980), pp. 17–55; José María Mínguez, "Ruptura social e implantación del feudalismo en el Noroeste peninsular (siglos VIII–X)," *Studia Historica. Historia Medieval* 3/2 (1985), 7–32.

[10]Pascual Martínez Sopena and María José Carbajo Serrano, "Notas sobre la colonización de Tierra de Campos en el siglo X: Villobera," in *El pasado histórico de Castilla y León. I. Edad media* (Burgos, 1983), pp. 113–25; and Pascual Martínez Sopena, *La Tierra de Campos Occidental. Poblamiento, poder y comunidad del siglo X al XIII* (Valladolid, 1985).

which family farms were changing hands constantly. When necessary, communities defended their boundaries in court against neighbors or local powers such as the monasteries. In some regions this was also the network used by public authorities for the purpose of imposing taxes or political control over population, and the like.[11]

Names of Peasants and Names of Nobles

Compared with peasants, the choice of a name was much more meaningful for aristocrats. Many examples prove that the name for the newborn was a sort of political program established by the family for that child. Parents were aware of the importance of such a choice. From the tenth century on, wills from Catalan aristocracy give interesting evidence about expectations for the newborns. Some of these wills provided legacies for the babies still to be born, and others were written while the wives were still pregnant. It is easy to imagine how pressing this could be when the family had no sons. In one of these, a Catalan *miles* writes in his will: "*Item dimito illum pregnatum quem uxor mea portat in eius chausimento, et si filius erit dono ei totum honorem meum de Dalfiano inperpetuum post hobitum matris eius et vocetur Berengarius.*"[12] This instance is quite unusual in showing that the name was the father's choice, and that naming was so important that it had to be determined in advance in his will. The lack of further examples makes it impossible to say whether this was a normal practice or exceptional behavior.

---

[11]Roger Collins, "Visigothic Law and Regional Custom in Disputes in Early Medieval Spain," in *The Settlement of Disputes in Early Medieval Europe*, ed. Wendy Davies and Paul Fouracre (Cambridge, 1986), pp. 85–104. Concerning the importance of *villa* as the basic structure of rural society, see Juan José Larrea, *La Navarre du IVe au XIIe siècle. Peuplement et société* (Brussels, 1998), especially pp. 163–211, 255–58, and 323–26.

[12]Biblioteca de Cataluña, perg. Vilabertran 9981, Will of Guillem de Vilarig, year 1208. *Regestum* in Josep M. Marquès, *Escriptures de Santa Maria de Vilabetran (968–1300)* (Figueres, 1995), p. 293, document number 734.

From the tenth century on, Spanish noble families promoted the adoption of a two-element naming system involving the addition of the patronym as a second element. In the central part of the country, in Navarra and Rioja, the change to double names had started long before this. As early as the tenth century, the majority of the men mentioned in charters bears a double name, as can be seen in the documents from the monasteries of Leyre and San Millán de la Cogolla.[13] But the reasons for such an exceptionally early adoption of double names remain still to be explained.

High proportions of people in neighboring areas were also using a double-naming pattern prior to the eleventh century. But the change toward the double-name pattern spread later in northwestern Spain than in Navarra and Rioja. Even in literary sources that deal with people living in both these regions at the same time, it is possible to notice that the double-name pattern was commonly in use in the Pyrenees, while westwards, in Asturias, the single name was still the dominant practice.[14]

During the first decades of the eleventh century, eastern regions like Catalonia or Aragón also adopted the double-name system. More precisely, in Catalonia the years 1030–50 are those in which a single-name system was replaced by that of double names.[15] But the adoption of the double-name pattern was not uniform at all levels of society. Almost everywhere peasant families were more reluctant to use this new pattern. If we consider them separately the evidence concerning nobles and peasants

---

[13]García de Cortázar, "Antroponimia en Navarra y Rioja en los siglos X a XII," in Luis Suárez Fernández et al., *Estudios de Historia Medieval. Homenaje a Luis Suárez* (Valladolid, 1991), pp. 175–91.

[14]See the case of the Chronicle of Alfonso III in Pascual Martínez Sopena, "L'anthroponymie de l'Espagne chrétienne entre le IXe et le XIIe siècle," in *L'anthroponymie. Document de l'histoire sociale*, ed. Bourin, Martin, and Menant, pp. 63–85; and contributions from Galicia, Bierzo, and León in *Antroponimia y sociedad*, ed. Martínez Sopena.

[15]Enric Moreu-Rey, "Consideracions sobre l'antroponímia dels segles X i XI," *Miscel·lània Antoni M. Badia i Margarit* 3, *Estudis de llengua i literatura catalanes* 11 (Barcelona, 1985), pp. 5–44; and Michel Zimmermann, "Les débuts de la 'révolution anthroponymique' en Catalogne, Xe–XIIe siècles," *Annales du Midi* 102 (1990), 289–308.

shows a striking contrast nearly everywhere. In Navarra where double names were widespread already in the tenth century, some peasants still bear a single name around 1000, and their stock of names is larger than that of the nobles of the same period.[16] In early samples from Castille, the double-name pattern is clearly in advance among the noble families, and a majority of peasants are referred to with a single name while most of the aristocrats use the patronym.[17]

A similar phenomenon appears in Liébana, León, Bierzo, and Galicia. In all these regions charters show clearly that an important part of the peasant population is still designated with single names after the year 1000, and that the change to the double-name pattern had started earlier among aristocracy.[18] In the Catalan counties peasant families also adopt the new system somewhat later and in some places they keep using the single-name pattern until well after 1200, whereas aristocratic families clearly had already adopted the double-name pattern.

It is not easy to explain why peasants were more attached to single names or why aristocrats adopted the double name sooner. In the tenth and eleventh centuries the double name was always formed with the addition of the name of the father, a patronym, as the second element. So this means that noble families were stressing filiation. This change is also related to a change in the stock of names with the introduction of new ones of Christian origin that gained popular favor very quickly and rapidly reduced the total number of different names in use. Names like *Peter* or *John* for men or *Mary* for women seem to have been preferred while

---

[16]Larrea, *La Navarre*, pp. 320–22.

[17]Ernesto Pastor Díaz de Garayo, *Castilla en el tránsito de la Antigüedad al Feudalismo. Poblamiento, poder político y estructura social del Arlanza al Duero (siglos VIII–XI)* (Valladolid, 1996), p. 271.

[18]See especially the contributions of Ermelindo Portela Silva, María Carmen Pallares Mendez, Marta González Vázquez, Francisco Javier Pérez Rodríguez, María Carmen Rodríguez González, and Mercedes Durany Castrillo on monastic archives from Galicia that provide comparative tables in *Antroponimia y sociedad*, ed. Martínez Sopena.

people abandoned some of the Germanic, Latin, or pre-Roman names. These changes could be understood as part of a broad cultural renewal, but at the same time they could have been the result of the restriction of each family's stock of usable names. Noble families may have led the process by restricting the stock of names used for their sons or simply by being more careful about their choices. The father's or grandfather's names were being more frequently chosen than those of more distant kin. This was also a way of stressing filiation over broader kinship networks as, undoubtably, was the adoption of patronyms. At the same time in some communities the "elites" were called the *filii bene natorum* or *filii bonorum hominum*. These expressions undoubtedly refer to the wealthy people who received some kind of privilege or access to some special functions (i.e., military services). But as these terms suggest, such a social differentiation was justified through family descent. In other words, patronyms become more relevant because of individuals' claims on collective privileges or functions restricted to some special groups.[19]

Peasants could be compelled to adopt double-name patterns for similar reasons, and not just because of the cultural influence of noble families over peasant communities. Still, in many regions in the eleventh century, rights and duties of each individual man or woman depended on residence in a particular village. Inheritance was less important for them than it was for the wealthy nobles. This may be one reason why peasants adopted patronyms somewhat later than other social groups.

It can be useful to compare peasants' reluctance with that shown by clerics and women. Clerics continue to use the single-name pattern until late in the twelfth century, even if they usually added a functional adjunct like *presbiter* or *abbas* to their names. Obviously their links with their families were not completely cut off when they entered into the cloister or chapter, but they undoubtedly no longer maintained the same connections as their lay brothers and sisters. More interesting is the case of women, who

---

[19]This link has been pointed out by Martínez Sopena, "L'anthroponymie de l'Espagne chrétienne," p. 84.

seem also to have adopted the double-name pattern one or two generations later than men, especially in the regions of northwestern Spain, and much later in those of the northeast. Nevertheless, at the end of the twelfth century there was a sharp contrast between westerns regions like León or Galicia where a large majority of women used names with patronyms, and Catalonia or Aragón where such patronyms were held by a small minority of women. In these eastern regions around 90 percent of women were still referred to with a single name during the last third of the twelfth century. It is interesting to notice that this regional contrast resembles the one involving regions where women's rights were seriously undermined by the introduction of the Roman dowry. That is, women were gradually excluded from inheritance claims because they now received a dowry in exchange.[20]

On the other hand, in the western regions of the kingdom of Castile and León, succession practices remained more faithful to the Visigothic heritage, which called for equality for all sons and daughters. This does not mean that shares were always perfectly equal and in many ways women were obviously under the control of parents or husbands, but at least they were not excluded from the point of view of the rules of inheritance. Quite significantly, women kept their names with a patronym even after their marriage because they did not thereby lose their claims. So daughters had more interest in stressing their family descent throughout their lives.[21]

In the case of peasants, as in that of women or clerics, we are dealing with people who from a comparative point of view had fewer individual rights to inheritance. Their claims to succession were less meaningful, and particularly as a group they were not as concerned with calling attention to their family descent as a way of distinguishing themselves from other

---

[20]Martin Aurell, *Les noces du comte. Mariage et pouvoir en Catalogne (785–1213)* (Paris, 1995).

[21]Pascual Martínez Sopena, "Parentesco y poder en León durante el siglo XI. La 'Casata' de Alfonso Díaz," *Studia Historica. Historia Medieval* 5 (1987), 33–87, and "Relations de parenté et héritage wisigothique dans l'aristocratie du royaume de León au XIe siècle," in *L'Europe héritière de l'Espagne wisigothique*, ed. Fontaine and Pellistrandi (Madrid, 1992), pp. 315–24.

individuals. But this could also be simply the perspective of the scribes who drew up the charters, who of course were not peasants. Nonetheless, however tardily or incompletely, peasants adopted the double-name pattern, thus following the path of noble families. This was particularly true when patronyms were replaced by another kind of personal naming, that of family names passed down over the generations.

A Second Change in Personal Naming: Peasants Named after their Farms

In the Catalan counties and in the kingdom of Aragón during the twelfth century, an increasing number of people used a place name as a second element in their names. This new model was used by the majority of men in Catalonia from the middle of the twelfth century on, at the same time that the patronym was gradually abandoned. This second change was clearly introduced by noble families who began to take the name of a castle as a family name. This was directly related to the functions of a *castellan* as a key element in the organization of feudal authority. It may also be related to the way in which lordships based on castles were being incorporated into family patrimonies. This means that they could be passed down through inheritance, or at least this was what noble families claimed. So it is easy to understand the importance of associating family names with castles, seen as centers of power. Family names also spread in a context of the tightening of agnatic lineages, in which primogeniture became the preferred pattern for inheritance. The Catalan and the French aristocracy had much in common in this development. In some cases, a family allocated a castle to a younger son who then took its name instead of his father's and brother's, and then started a secondary branch of the family with a different name. So even if primogeniture was not always strictly followed, the connection between names and castles was still in effect.[22]

---

[22]Lídia Martínez Teixidó, "La antroponimia nobiliaria del condado de Pallars en los siglos XI y XII," in *Antroponímia y sociedad*, ed. Martínez Sopena, pp. 337–38.

These changes did not take place in northwestern Spain. Despite regional variations, the patronym as a second element in double names continued to be the usual pattern from Navarra to Portugal. Obviously there may not have been merely one, singular reason for this development. But with regard first of all to the social context, castles did not have the central role in power structures that they did in the Catalan counties.[23] Second, aristocratic kinship did not change into agnatic lineages as in the French model described by Georges Duby. All sons and daughters could have a claim on the inheritance instead of families practicing primogeniture. So kinship ties could be far more complex and extend to all sons and daughters and need not have been confined to a single line of descent.[24]

Let us now turn to the changes in personal naming for peasants after the eleventh century. In the Catalan counties they shared to some degree the same evolution as the aristocracy. Some of them still received only a single name in the charters as in the early Middle Ages. Others also adopted as a family name the name of a place that could be handed down from generation to generation. To think about a cultural influence from the upper levels of feudal society is all too easy to do. But peasants could also have adopted family names for reasons quite similar to those applying to the aristocracy.

In fact, by the end of the twelfth century, a growing number of peasants were holding farms (*mansum*) or tenements with perpetual rights that could be inherited. Even if lordship was very oppressive and severe restrictions were imposed on succession, peasants could not be easily removed from their homes. It is possible to find cases of remarkable stability over the centuries in the link between families and farms. In

---

[23]Larrea, *La Navarre*, pp. 352–54 and 364–65.

[24]Besides articles by Martínez Sopena cited above, see María Carmen Pallares and Ermelindo Portela, "Elementos para el análisis de la aristocracia alto-medieval de Galicia: parentesco y patrimonio," *Studia Historica. Historia Medieval* 5 (1987), 17–32, and "Aristocracia y sistema de parentesco en la Galicia de los siglos centrales de la Edad Media. El grupo de los Traba," *Hispania* 185 (1993), 823–40.

these circumstances it is not surprising that peasants were taking their farms' names as family names.

But stability was not only a right but also a duty, in that peasants were bound to the land, and this bond was considered characteristic of servitude. Peasants were obliged to commit themselves to live permanently on their farms. Their link with farms became so strong that if they wanted to leave they had to redeem themselves from personal servitude which was an otherwise hereditary condition. Redemption was usually granted after the paying of a redemption fee and was frequently attested to during the second half of the twelfth century. Lords probably agreed to people leaving as long as someone else continued to live on the farm. Later lords tried to prevent those who left from retaining some sort of rights over their farms.[25]

Throughout the counties of Catalonia we have evidence proving that lords wanted to keep personal control over the people who were living on their domains. Domains were organized in farms, and they were in fact the basic unit of lordship. In any case, if earlier records describe farms with nothing but the name of the tenant or the inhabitant, from the thirteenth century on farms also acquire a name of their own which they give, furthermore, to those who live on it or hold it.[26]

As in the case of the castles, farms took a central position in the organization of powers at a local level. In this context, peasants' families changed to new forms of structure and inheritance patterns. Evidence of patrilocal residence becomes more abundant as some charters begin to register agreements between fathers and sons that include the principle of primogeniture. These arrangements commonly took place at the wedding of the principal heir who was going to live with his parents after his marriage. It is not too adventurous to propose that the new family structures and inheritance regulations were going in the same direction as servitude

---

[25]Paul H. Freedman, *The Origins of Peasant Servitude in Medieval Catalonia* (Cambridge, 1991).

[26]A similar process in Gascony: Benoît Cursente, *Des maisons et des hommes. La Gascogne médiévale (XIe–XVe siècle)* (Toulouse, 1998), p. 155.

in the sense that patrilocal marriage was the best way of keeping the family tied to the farm.[27] We can hardly find a comparable development in other regions of northwestern Spain, even if long-term tenure was also granted to peasant families with restrictions that sometimes entered into the category of what we call servitude.[28]

It may seem a paradox that the bondage of a son to the land was assuring the continuity of the family: his brothers and sisters were, after being freed, often expelled to growing towns or territories conquered from the Muslims. This mobility, which is the reverse side of the bondage of serfs to the land, may have been another factor encouraging the use of a place name as a family name. In Catalonia in particular, the one who left the farm could change his name if through marriage he came into the possession of another farm, but he could preserve his name of origin if he settled in a town. On a much larger scale the same process affected all the new territories conquered after the end of the eleventh century in Aragón in the Valley of the Ebro, where place names commonly lay at the origin of family names.

The society of twelfth-century Spain was a more stratified and divided one. Ethnic groups, for example, were more clearly identified than ever before, and urban groups were taking on a new identity and self-consciousness. In this framework, succession was more and more important, not only for the inheritance of goods or property but also for the transmission of status, of craft abilities, or of functions. Names were becoming a powerful tool for classifying people and assigning them to the place that destiny was supposed to have reserved for them.

---

[27]Lluís To Figueras, *Família i hereu a la Catalunya nord-oriental (segles X–XII)* (Barcelona, 1997).

[28]Liébana is the only region to the west of the Ebro where peasant families frequently use a place name as an element of their names, and also as a third element added after the patronym before 1200. See Julia Montenegro Valentín, "Antroponimia lebaniega en los siglos IX a XII," in *Antroponimia y sociedad*, ed. Martínez Sopena, pp. 181–203.

Personal Naming and Kinship in the Spanish Aristocracy

Pascual Martínez Sopena

Introduction

In recent years, a group of Spanish historians has been working on the medieval personal names project supervised by Monique Bourin. Our contributions dealing with the naming system in Christian Spain are grouped mainly into two recent studies. For this we have analyzed many diplomatic sources for the period from the ninth to the thirteenth centuries. In our conclusions we have highlighted the distinctive features of the naming system in central and western Spain on the one hand, and eastern regions, in particular Catalonia, on the other. From the twelfth century onward, the latter area shows a number of trends in common with the south of France, in the same way that the former displays its own common elements, the most significant being the strict observance of the system of *nomina paterna*, in evidence from the tenth century onwards.

The subject that I shall present here is related to these studies. Nevertheless, there are also certain differences. As suggested by the title of my own paper, I shall focus on the characteristics of anthroponomy among the nobility, concentrating on the central and western regions of Spain. I shall approach the theme by presenting three different and chronologically arranged pictures that will be drawn from three genealogical documents dating from the twelfth to the fourteenth centuries.

The first of these documents is the *Historia Roderici*, where one can find the genealogy of Rodrigo Díaz de Vivar, El Cid Campeador. The second comes from a genealogical record from the Patrons of the Monastery of Ferreira de Pallares, as recorded in the mid-thirteenth century. The third forms part of the "Tratado de las Armas" and was written in the 1340s by Don Juan Manuel, the great Castilian writer of the time.

As can be seen, I will be using literary sources above all for the discussion of historical questions. The historical accuracy of this information may be the subject of debate, but nevertheless these sources are of particular interest to me because they offer a very tangible and ideal image of the onomastic behavior of different aristocratic families. That is to say, they show a theoretical representation of onomastic customs, but one that is directly related to reality.

Once these documents have been analyzed, I shall conclude with some hypotheses aimed at explaining how the differences expressed in these onomastic models show the development of family structures within the nobility.

The First Image

The second half of the eleventh century is a period full of interest for Spanish history. Of the figures from this period, Rodrigo Díaz, El Cid Campeador, occupies a privileged position. His fame as an invincible warrior, based on the evidence of several different sources among which is the so-called *Historia Roderici*, deserves special mention.

There is some debate as to when this long Latin account was written. Perhaps it was a few years after the protagonist's death, as claimed by Ramón Menendez Pidal and Richard A. Fletcher or possibly somewhat later, as in the opinion of Colin Smith, who concludes that it was the work of Bishop Berenguer of Salamanca.[1] In any case, the work as we know it was written during the mid-twelfth century, the period in which I wish to place this first image.

---

[1]Ramón Menéndez Pidal, *La España del Cid*, 4th ed. (Madrid, 1947). Critical commentaries and edition of the text in vol. 2, pp. 904–69. Richard A. Fletcher, *The Quest for El Cid* (London, 1989). Colin Smith, "A Conjecture about the Authorship of the *Historia Roderici*," *Journal of Hispanic Research* 2/8 (1994), 175–81.

The *Historia Roderici* begins with a genealogical record of the hero covering the previous seven generations, beginning with one Flainus Calvus. Rodrigo Díaz descends from the masculine line of one of his sons; it is also recorded that his great-grandfather had wed the great-granddaughter of another of Flainus Calvus's sons.

This genealogy presents problems of historical identification. According to tradition, as mentioned by the chroniclers of the thirteenth century, Flainus Calvus was one of the legendary judges of Castile in the ninth century. But this is from a very late and fragmentary source; the only significant fact to come out of it is that Flainus Calvus gave up the post for which he had been chosen by the Castilians. We know nothing of his supposed descendants until the first half of the eleventh century when two of Rodrigo Díaz's grandfathers, Flain Nuñez and Rodrigo Alvarez, appear in historical records. The latter, from the line of Rodrigo Díaz's mother, is mentioned with some frequency in the documents of King Fernando I; scholars agree that the maternal line of Rodrigo Díaz's family must have held a higher social position than that of his father, Diego Flainez.

Nevertheless, for our purposes the historical accuracy of the genealogy is less important than the onomastic structure of the *nobilissimi ac bellatoris viri prosapiam*. The most outstanding aspect of this text is that, for six generations, fathers gave their sons their own names by way of the *nomen paternum*. Furthermore, the repeated use of the earliest ancestor's name would have assured in the male line of El Cid a certain element of identification in alternation with the patronymic derived from it (*Flainus/ Flainez*). Although it is obvious that the author gave pride of place to the masculine ascendancy of Rodrigo Díaz and to the internal coherence of his onomastic model, the names of other male family members mentioned in the text show the same pattern; this means that each descendant received the *nomen paternum* added to his own personal name and that a hereditary "family name" simply did not exist. There is, moreover, another point of interest: the granting of the name "Rodrigo" to the future Campeador, which broke a well-established sequence, was dictated by the importance of his maternal relatives.

What interests us, therefore, is not the accuracy of the data, but the expression of a predetermined model of name election. Now, why should we speak of a model? To what degree was this applied generally both in space and time? Of course, the information that we have highlighted corresponds very well with what is known of naming practices of the aristocracy in northwestern Spain in the tenth, eleventh, and twelfth centuries. The situation of the eastern territories was quite different in the twelfth century. The very same *Historia Roderici* presents some of these differences with other authors (I refer to Carlos Laliena and Lluís To Figueras, who have studied it in depth). In fact, the chronicle identifies Aragonese nobles with a more complex system of references, which adds a place name to the *nomen paternum* and vacillates between the use of the *nomen paternum* (or perhaps better, the *nombre vinculado*, to use Lydia Martinez's terminology) and a name that denotes place of origin when referring to the Catalonian nobles, the "*francos*" of that text.

Naturally, the *Historia* offers complementary readings. For example, the only male who does not have his own *nomen paternum* is the first of the line, Flainus Calvus, but this happens in all the cases in which we have been able to reconstruct the line of descent for relatives back to the ninth or the beginning of the tenth century.[2] The whole picture also offers some important gaps, particularly with regard to the female forebears. The few women mentioned are identified not through their names but thanks to explanations about their fathers and brothers. This usage stands in sharp contrast to that of diplomatic sources of the mid-twelfth century, in which the majority of Castilian women are named by the use of the *nomen* + *nomen paternum*.

---

[2]For a hypothesis with regard to the nickname Calvus borne by this Flainus, it is as well to remember one of Michael Mitterauer's general observations: this nickname denotes the condition of being tonsured, that is to say, of being a clergyman. Perhaps this fact could be linked to his having given up the post of judge, according to the tradition as described previously; in this case, the name may offer additional information not presented by the writers of the time. Of course, all of this depends on an evaluation of the tradition involved and not the debatable historical reality.

Second Image

Our second representation comes from the middle of the thirteenth century and is based upon the analysis of a document from the Monastery of Ferreira de Pallares in Galicia. This document is an extensive genealogical record covering more than three centuries. It begins with the monastery's founder, Count Ero, who was alive at the start of the tenth century—and goes right up to the Patrons of the Monastery of Ferreira at the time when the document was written. Some fifty names are mentioned in the source. Each name generally designates a member of the family, man or woman; only a few of the names are not personal ones, since they serve as a collective reference to small groups of close relatives. Thus the documents of Ferreira de Pallares transmit an image or picture that can be compared in some respects with that of the genealogy of Rodrigo Díaz. Just as in that one, there is a predominance of the forms of *nomen + nomen paternum*. This latter element, the *nomen paternum*, invariably preserves the living character that it already had in the mid-twelfth century and for a long time before. That is to say, it had not become fossilized and was not passed on as a family name.[3]

But there are also two important innovations with regard to the genealogy of El Cid. The first is that for most women, a common norm is followed, *nomen + nomen paternum*. This fact is reassuring since it shows that the system of female names was not different from that of male ones. It is worth adding that diplomatic sources from the twelfth and thirteenth centuries confirm this point of view in the western territories of Spain.

In this respect, the differences between this text and the genealogy of El Cid have a possible explanation. The author of El Cid's genealogy highlights his lineage, using the very term *stirpis* to designate it. That is to say, his main concern was the masculine ascendancy of the hero: the women

---

[3]Jaime de Salazar Acha, "Los descendientes del conde Ero Fernández, fundador del monasterio de Santa María de Ferreira de Pallares," in *Galicia en la Edad Media* (Madrid, 1990), pp. 67–86.

mentioned serve only to reinforce the nobility of El Cid's origins. If the *Historia Roderici* was written by Bishop Berenguer, a Catalonian cleric, this genealogical selection might be an echo of the male-based practices of twelfth-century Catalonian society. In contrast to this, the author of the Ferreira account wished to indicate the origins of the rights of patrons in the thirteenth century. Greater importance was given to women as heirs and as the means for the transmission of rights, in accordance with the customs of the Kingdoms of Castile and León.

The second innovation is that in the generation of the late twelfth and early thirteenth centuries, other supplementary data appear in the form of complex names. Together with the traditional form of *nomen + nomen paternum*, a third element is added: a place name or a nickname. As the thirteenth century progresses, this latter characteristic becomes more and more common and diverse. Used as a collective reference, as described before, these place names or nicknames even come to replace individual names; it can also be seen that some people, with what appears to be a *nomen paternum*, are really using a true "family name." This fact is very significant. Although the traditional patterns retain their prestige, they co-exist with other practices, which stress the formation of distinctive groups and their public recognition expressed through this additional nickname.

It is appropriate here to add a further explanation. The persons or groups mentioned in the records of the Patrons of the Monastery of Ferreira with an additional name (place name, nickname, old *nomen paternum*), belonged to diverse groups within the aristocracy. Several of them must have been members of the middle level of the Galician and Castilian nobility (Tavoada, Burrageros, Orvanega). Others belonged to the higher strata of the Castilian and Leonese aristocracy (Cameros, Girón, Ponce). The conclusion to be drawn from such a trend is clear: by the mid-thirteenth century a new tendency had arisen among the aristocracy of the kingdom that gave importance to additional names as identifying elements for a group of relatives.

Third Image

For our third and last image we shall use another text dating from the first half of the fourteenth century. This is to be found among the manuscripts of Don Juan Manuel, the great Castilian writer and statesman of the time. Toward the end of his life, perhaps in 1342, Don Juan Manuel wrote his "Tratado" or "Libro de Armas." In this work there is a description of the history of his family taken from several different sources. It is a kind of memorandum of the family line. To begin, he tells of how his father, the Infante Don Manuel, received his name.[4]

The Infante Don Manuel was the youngest son of the marriage between Fernando III of Castile and Beatriz of Swabia. While still expecting, Queen Beatriz had a premonition in a dream of the glory to which her future son was destined; in the words of Don Juan Manuel, "thanks to that child and his lineage, the death of Christ will be avenged." Once the boy was born, his parents consulted the bishop of Segovia in order to choose an appropriate name and they described the dream to him. The bishop decided that the ideal name would be "Manuel," which contains two things, the first being that it is one of the names of God and the second that it signifies "God with us."

The form of this tale is associated with a long tradition; one only has to remember the gospel account of the naming of John the Baptist. But most important for our argument is that this constitutes the starting point in the recorded memory of the lineage. By associating this choice with providential circumstances, Don Juan Manuel bestows some mystical property on the name received by his father. Acquiring this symbolic content, it is not unusual that "Manuel" becomes a name distinctive of the descendants of the Infante. In the case of the very same Don Juan Manuel or of his brother Sancho Manuel, one might think of a typical *nomen paternum*; but it can be seen that the sons and successors of both of them adopted it in a general manner.

---

[4]Andrés Giménez Soler, *Don Juan Manuel. Biografía y Estudio crítico* (Zaragoza, 1932), pp. 677–91.

It is very important to add that the "Tratado de las Armas" receives its name from the attention that it gives to the Shield of Arms awarded to his son, Manuel, by Fernando III. There are also extensive references to the former bishop of Segovia, now the archbishop of Seville. Approached by the king who chose an appropriate moment to ask him about the elements that should compose Infante Manuel's coat of arms, the ecclesiastic made a proposition that was accepted immediately. The most distinctive element of the Coat of Arms of the Infante shows a winged hand (*mano alada*) brandishing a sword.

Don Juan Manuel offers broad and conventional explanations for the symbolism of the shield of arms. He also alludes to the imperial blood of Swabia and Byzantium, coming from Queen Beatriz. For the same reasons for which "Manuel" became the additional name for those of this line, this coat of arms was to be transmitted within the descendants of the Infante for centuries to come.

To summarize, the "Tratado de las Armas" is an exercise in the historical records of a family group. But the mythification of the name of its founder and the association between the name and the characteristic shield indicates a new awareness about these two systems of signs, the name and the heraldic emblem. Fortunately, this new awareness found its expression in an illustrious member of the lineage, perhaps the most outstanding of the era's Castilian writers. I wish to stress that, from the point of view of my arguments, perhaps his greatest merit is his capacity to adequately express a sensitivity common to the Castilian nobility of that same period.

Reflections

From these three images a certain evolution can be deduced in the customs of aristocratic naming. Our objective is to put these naming customs into their family contexts. In what way? Recently, our colleague Robert Durand carried out a very interesting study, in which he associated naming practices and inheritance customs in the western Mediterranean between the eleventh and thirteenth centuries. Durand detects a correlation between the use of the system of *nomina paterna* and the presence of bilinear family groups. This fact is characteristic of the western regions of the Iberian Peninsula and it contrasts with Catalonia, the Languedoc, and Italian areas where there seems to be a dominance of patrilineal descent groups in the transmission of property and inheritance.[5]

In effect, our survey shows the same trend. At the beginning of the twelfth century, families were groups of relatives without a strict notion of vertical lineage. Even in the case of Rodrigo Díaz de Vivar, the maintenance of one name down through the generations (*Flaín, Flaínez*) is not incompatible with the adoption of other names that come from the maternal, and possibly more illustrious, branch of the family. The additional names that may be found ("Campi Doctori") seem to be purely personal.

At that time the transmission of inheritance did not favor one, single individual but all the sons. This custom was still observed in the thirteenth century. As I have already said, the genealogical records of the Monastery of Ferreira are good evidence of how women and men shared hereditary rights, thus creating an extensive network of heirs.

Nevertheless, this situation was not unalterable. In the thirteenth century one could perceive certain elements of change. From the point of view of personal names, there already existed surnames that were not personal: they were linked to a particular ancestor and were inherited from him, or they were associated with the territorial domain characteristic of a limited group of relatives. These surnames might accompany the traditional name, *nomen + nomen paternum*. However, one can observe that some of the sons received the father's entire name. These different systems co-existed at the beginning of the fourteenth century, but the sophisticated explanation of Don Juan Manuel indicates a new assessment of the name as one of the distinctive elements of what was already known as *linaje*.

---

[5]Robert Durand, "Surnoms et structures de la famille," in *L'anthroponymie. Document de l'histoire sociale des mondes méditerranéens médiévaux*, ed. Monique Bourin, Jean-Marie Martin, and François Menant, Collections de l'École française de Rome 226 (Rome, 1996), p. 418.

Furthermore, the striking link of the name with the coat of arms must not be forgotten.

If we move on to the area of succession customs, we observe that there were parallel changes at the same time. The institution of the *mayorazgo*, characterized by strict rules of the transference of the greater part of the estate to a single heir, was emerging in Castile. This can be seen in those created by Alfonso Martínez de Olivera in 1302 and by Blasco Muñoz in 1320, which may be considered to be two of the earliest known cases. Although there is no mention of the term *mayorazgo*, something very similar is contained in the will of Don Juan Manuel, which must date from around 1345; this great writer had a number of sons and daughters, but the most important share of his property was passed on to his son Fernando Manuel. Nevertheless, this evolution was far from being complete. We have no evidence of the establishment of *mayorazgos* in general until the end of the fourteenth century; it is also at that moment when some of the *mayorazgos* stated that heirs had to keep the additional name (already a true surname) and the arms of their founder.[6]

To conclude: the traditions and changes in naming customs give an idea of the attitudes of the family group which, as we have seen, imposed themselves, for example, on the customs of patrimonial inheritance. Still, as the data confirm, in Castile there seems to have been a long period of transition during the late Middle Ages. In any case, there was an ideological atmosphere favorable to these which had by then, within the Castilian aristocracy, long since been consolidated in the eastern regions, particularly in Catalonia.

---

[6]Isabel Beceiro Pita and Ricardo Córdoba, *Parentesco, poder y mentalidad. La nobleza castellana, siglos XII–XV* (Madrid, 1990).

FAMILY MEMORY AND THE DURABILITY OF THE *NOMEN PATERNUM*

Robert Durand

The following reflections come from a careful study of Portuguese anthroponomy as found in several different sources: cartularies, genealogical charts, and royal inquests.[1] The latter of these have brought to light the reliance, for over half a millennium, on a naming system based on the widespread use of the father's name, from one generation to the next, as a surname for all of the children; this practice will be referred to here as the *nomen paternum*.[2]

The problems that this custom creates for the maintenance of family memory are well known. The regular repetition of the father's name from one generation to the next makes possible a horizontal representation of the family but rules out a vertical one. The question is then to determine whether in regions that favored this system over the long term, people neglected the family memory in the vertical or long sense in favor of

---

[1] Cartularies: *Livro Preto da Sé de Coimbra*, ed. Arquivo da Universidade de Coimbra, 3 vols. (Coimbra, 1977–79); *Le cartulaire Baio-Ferrado du monastère de Grijó, XIe–XIIIe siècles*, ed. Robert Durand (Paris, 1971); *O mosteiro de Arouca do século X ao século XIII*, ed. Maria Helena da Cruz Coelho (Coimbra, 1977). Genealogical charts: *Livros velhos de Linhagens*, ed. Joseph Piel and José Mattoso (Lisbon, 1980); *Livro de Linhagens do Conde D. Pedro*, ed. José Mattoso (Lisbon, 1980). Royal inquests: *Portugaliae Monumenta Historica. Inquisitiones*.

[2] Scholars understand the term *nomen paternum* in different ways. Some see it as a naming practice that involves giving an individual his father's name (in the genitive or in the nominative) as a surname. Others view it as the surname alone so long as it is based on the father's name. Semantically the latter is doubtless more justified. Nonetheless I take the first approach; for me *nomen paternum* means the combination of name plus surname.

realizing other objectives, or whether the system did not at the same time make available other ways of maintaining it over time. Before evoking the different representations of the family brought about by the use of the *nomen paternum*, I think it is necessary to call attention to the evidence for its durability over several centuries in Portugal.

The Evidence

The study of the *nomen paternum* in Portugal begins in the last decade of the eleventh century. It was then that a two-element naming system won out definitively over the use of a single name, with chronological variations in different regions not exceeding a quarter of a century.[3] From this perspective, Portugal was not a European land's end, receiving at a later date influences radiating out from a hypothetical center. A fine series of studies by Spanish colleagues[4] focusing on different parts of the Iberian Peninsula (Pascual Martínez Sopena gave a magisterial synthesis of these at the Rome colloquium[5]) have shown that the passage to a two-element naming system took place everywhere at about the same time. This leads me to confirm (with reference to Martínez Sopena's study), that viewed in all its different elements, the Portuguese anthroponymic system does not stand out as a distinctive one, but in fact conforms to the naming practices of all of the rest of the central and western parts of the Iberian

---

[3]Robert Durand, "Données anthroponymiques du *Livro Preto de la Cathédrale de Coïmbre*," in *Genèse médiévale de l'anthroponymie moderne* (= GMAM), *I. Études d'anthroponymie médiévale Ie et IIe rencontres, Azay-le-Ferron 1986 et 1987*, ed. Monique Bourin (1990), pp. 219–32; Matthieu Brossaud, "Les exemples portugais de Grijó et d'Arouca (Xe–XIIIe siecles)" (M.A. thesis, Univ. of Nantes, 1990).

[4]*Antroponomia y sociedad. Sistemas de identificación hispano-cristianos en los siglos IX a XIII*, ed. Pascual Martínez Sopena (Santiago de Compostela-Valladolid, 1995).

[5]Pascual Martínez Sopena, "L'anthroponymie de l'Espagne chrétienne entre le IXe et le XIIIe siècles," in *L'anthroponymie. Document de l'histoire sociale des mondes méditerranéens médiévaux*, ed. Monique Bourin, Jean-Marie Martin, and François Menant (Rome, 1996), pp. 63–85.

Peninsula. Having stated this I will now summarize my findings under three different headings.[6]

The Use of the *Nomen Paternum*:
The Nucleus of an Entire Naming System

From the time when double names became more numerous than single ones, surnames (the second name) taken from personal names (i.e., anthroponymic surnames) accounted for anywhere from 74 to 90 percent of all in that category (variations according to different regions and time periods). These surnames were always written in the genitive case, or in a form thereof. One of the rare names not affected by this was the Basque name *Garcia*, never found in the genitive form. Arabic names borne by *mozarabs* were easily latinized: *Omar* became *Omari* or *Omariz*, and *Zoleiman* became *Zoleimaniz*, just as readily as *Petrus* or *Suarius*. In some instances, the genitive case admitted certain variants. *Didacus* thus became, successively, *Didaci, Didazi, Didaz*, and *Diaz*. Sometimes the genitive was affected by the Arabic *ibn*: thus the *Egas* were at first called *Ibn Egas*, then the name was contracted into *Ibeniegas, Benegas, Beniegas*, then *Venegas* and finally *Viegas*. This takes into account only the commonest forms; in the single cartulary source of these examples there are in all thirteen different variants of the term.[7] Over against this mass of names in the genitive case, the use of the nominative to form these surnames is exceptional and affects only a few, such as *Fafes* and *Cesar*, and even the latter appears more frequently in the genitive.

---

[6]These comments summarize the conclusions of several studies that cite the documentary evidence on which they are based, specifically, Robert Durand, "Le système anthroponymique portugais (région du Bas-Douro) du Xe au XIIIe siècle," in *Antroponimia y sociedad*, ed. Martínez Sopena, pp. 103–20, and "Trois siècles de dénomination aristocratique portugaise d'après la littérature généalogique," in GMAM, *III. Enquêtes généalogiques et données prosopographiques*, ed. Monique Bourin and Pascal Chareille (1995), pp. 43–54.

[7]*O mosteiro de Arouca*, ed. Coelho, index of names, pp. 411-57.

The Genitive Case Designates the Progenitor

The apparent tautology of this heading is called for in order to distinguish between Portuguese or west Iberian practices and those of certain other regions. All the checks that can be made through fragmentary genealogies reconstructed from cartulary evidence, or from the rich and plentiful genealogical literature of the thirteenth and fourteenth centuries, are in agreement that all anthroponymic surnames are patronyms in the first sense of that term, i.e., are names of the father. The countercheck to this is the fact that all the children of the same father, boys and girls, have the same surname. Indeed it is to be noted that throughout these documents there is an insistence on repeating the surname for each of the children even in large families (for instance, the nine children of Fromarigus Suariz and Elvira Nuniz, each of whom is so named in the opening and closing part of the document, and this despite the length of their surname, Fromariguiz).[8] In passing, I would call attention to the fact that there is no gender bias in this naming system. Masculine and feminine naming practices evolved in the same rhythm with regard both to the transition from single to double (complex) names and to the use of the *nomen paternum*.

The System Takes Hold over a Long Period

It is well known that certain regions (the Languedoc of Monique Bourin and the Catalonia of Lluís To Figueras) had recourse to the *nomen paternum* system in a systematic fashion for only a few decades, or at the most several generations, in particular at the time of the development of complex naming, but then abandoned it.[9] This evolution was very different

---

[8] *Le cartulaire Baio-Ferrado*, ed. Durand.

[9] Monique Bourin, "Les formes anthroponymiques et leur évolution d'après les données du cartulaire du chapitre cathédral d'Agde (Xe–1250)," in GMAM I, ed. Bourin, pp. 178–217; Lluís To Figueras, "Antroponimia de los condados catalanes (Barcelona, Girona y Osona, siglos X–XIII)," in *Antroponimia y sociedad*, ed. Martínez Sopena, pp. 371–94. See also

in Portugal where the system was in effect until at least the fifteenth century ("at least" is a confession of my ignorance about later centuries). In any case, for the fifteenth century, the lists of tenant farmers of Alcobaça studied by Iria Gonçalves[10] leave no room for doubt; there was no guarantee that the same surname would still be passed down over several generations. This obviously does not amount to archaic practices in naming; as studies of Italian naming have shown,[11] the adoption of hereditarily transmittable family names did not depend on economic trends or urban expansion. This leads to the inference that the use of the *nomen paternum* was the result of a choice, and this quite obviously was directly related to certain conceptions of the family without which there could be no explanation for the persistence of the former over time. But which conception of the family?

Conceptions of the Family

At first glance, the *nomen paternum* system gives only a momentary glimpse or snapshot of the family, a generational conception. To gain a fuller view of it calls for additional information, such as references to the place or function or sobriquet of the person in question, or the choice of a limited number of first names from the family stock of names. These combinations can lead to three more or less explicit conceptions of the family.

Michel Zimmermann, "Les débuts de la révolution anthroponymique en Catalogne (Xe–XIIe siècles)," in Charles Higounet, Pierre Bonnassie, and Jean-Bernard Marquette, eds., *Cadres de vie et société dans le Midi médiéval,* Annales du Midi 102 (Toulouse, 1990), pp. 289–308.

[10]Iria Gonçalves, "Antroponimia das terras alcobacenses nos fins da Idade Média," *Do Tempo e da História* 5 (1972), 159–200.

[11]See *Genèse médiévale de l'anthroponymie moderne. L'espace italien,* ed. François Menant and Jean-Marie Martin (Rome, 1994–95), pp. 723–36.

Brothers and Sisters Have Equal Rights of Inheritance

The attribution of the same surname to all the children of the same father makes it possible to identify easily the brothers and the sisters. This is all the more true in that all of the children, regardless of their social status or sex, keep this identity for the rest of their lives, even if in the case of the aristocracy, some add to their surname a toponymic element, often connected with a function or office (administrator, or *tenens*, of land; but since this function is not hereditary the third name is no more transmittable than is the second). In the case of the daughters marriage does not affect their names.

This situation has to be put into perspective with the inheritance system in effect in Portugal until at least the end of the thirteenth century. It must also be seen in light of To Figueras's comments about eleventh century Catalonia: he correctly asserts that "the patronym makes it possible to create an egalitarian link between all of the sons and their father," and this enables them "to identify themselves with their father and thus claim his succession."[12] The only reservation I would have to this generalization is that in Portugal people sometimes named one of the sons, apparently the eldest, after the father (e.g., *Petrus Petri*) and thus departed from the strict equality of children vis-à-vis the father. Apart from this, medieval Portugal remained faithful to the Visigothic tradition of equal division of the family patrimony among all the children, including daughters. The documentary record provides abundant proof of this. I will cite two examples.

It happens frequently that a religious establishment to which someone has bequeathed his inheritance *pro anima* (for the salvation of his soul) seeks to buy the other parts of the same property from the other co-heirs. In such cases the purchase price paid for the other parts or shares is always strictly the same. This rule has such force that the *boni homines* of the village are pledges for its observance. Conversely, in the case of an inadvertent

---

[12]Lluís To Figueras, "Anthroponymie et pratiques successorales," in *L'anthroponymie. Document de l'histoire sociale*, ed. Bourin et al., p. 427.

unequal division of the family inheritance (paternal or maternal), the same *boni homines* can intervene at the time of the division of the second inheritance in order to reestablish the equilibrium to the advantage of the heirs victimized by the first division.[13]

The Kindred as Guardian of the Family Honor and Its Interests

The *nomen paternum*, and its corollary, the absence of a family name, also makes possible the direct identification of uncles and paternal aunts. But this does not mean the maternal branch is invisible, since, as already noted, the mother keeps her name for her entire life. Moreover, it can happen that the mother's surname, that is, the maternal grandfather's name, is given as the name to one of the children.[14] Now as studies of Emma Montanos Ferrín,[15] among others, have shown, the two branches of the kingroup can be led to intervene collectively to assure the guardianship of orphans. In effect, if the care of the child is always left to the surviving parent, father or mother, the economic supervision of his goods continues to be the responsibility either of both branches or of the one offering the most guarantees. This is also true for the marriage of orphans; in addition to getting the authorization of the surviving parent, it is also necessary to have that of the kinsmen of the other branch, all the more reason why consent comes from both sides when both the father and mother are deceased.[16]

---

[13]Robert Durand, *Les campagnes portugaises entre Douro et Tage aux XIIe et XIIIe siècles* (Paris, 1982), p. 116.

[14]To give an example, there was the family that was patron of the collegiate church of Grijo. The eldest son of Fromarigus Suariz and Elvira Nuniz received the name *Nunus*, or that of his maternal grandfather. As eldest son, his full name, *Nunus Fromariguiz*, commemorated both his father's and his mother's families.

[15]Emma Montanos Ferrín, *La familia en la Alta Edad Media española* (Pamplona, 1980), p. 73.

[16]Ferrín, *La familia*, p. 42.

Concerns about preserving family honor are no different than those regarding economic interests. In the Estremadura of Leon, for instance, a group of laws codified in the twelfth century (and, to be sure, often called archaic), grants vengeance in case of dishonor due to rape, abduction, or indecent exposure, to both sides of the kin group.[17]

Having said this, the *nomen paternum* is nonetheless oriented to descendants in the male line. But to situate the bearer of such a name in relation to his ancestors, he must be given a first name already borne regularly by them, or what Christiane Klapisch-Zuber calls a "family first name." It is in this way that the remembrance of ancestors can be kept alive.

Remembrance of the Ancestors?

It seems indeed that this is of only secondary concern compared to the preoccupations I have just evoked, that is, respect for the equality of brothers and sisters and the need for the preceding generation to look after the interests of the younger generation. Having said this, it turns out that certain names are preferred in certain families, and that these could serve to single out given lineages. There are several examples of this in the *Livros de Linhagens*, and the fragmentary genealogies that can be reconstituted from the cartularies confirm this practice. In fact there are several strategies for maintaining the remembrance of ancestors. The most unmistakable involves giving the eldest son the name of the paternal grandfather. This system is particularly striking for the modern observer when the names repeated from grandfather to grandson are unusual or rare ones. Thus, in the *Livros de Linhagens,* the descendants of a certain Fafes Sarracins can be followed through seven generations through the intermediary of his eldest son Godinho Fafes; the regular alternation from generation to generation of the names *Fafes* and *Godinho* gives a succession of *nomina paterna* in Godinho Fafes and Fafes Godins which makes possible the identification of the family of the Godinhos over the long term. In this case, as Céline

[17]Ferrín, *La familia,* p. 132.

Perol has noted for Tuscany, the repetition of first names points to a "biological journey through a vast ancestry."[18] A second and less obvious practice involved the massive though less regular repetition of several dominant names.

It may well have been this concern to draw upon patrimonial or family names that explains the determined resistance to the christianization of name stocks. The evidence in fact shows a remarkable persistence of Germanic names such as *Menendus, Gundisalvus, Suarius,* still in use in Portugal today, in the face of the Christian *Peter*s and *John*s.

Nonetheless a close study of the *Livres de Lignages* does not bring to light any universally applicable rules for naming children: we must recognize that in many lineages, the family reasons for the choice of names are completely lost to us.

Conclusion

Faced with the systematic use of the *nomen paternum* from the eleventh century on, and the perpetuation of this practice at least to the end of the Middle Ages, the desire of families to keep their memory alive appears to have been drawn in several directions, sometimes almost to the point of self-contradiction. A direct reading of the evidence makes possible the identification of two generations, at least in part: the younger generation of brothers and sisters who are heirs on a basis of equality to the family patrimony, and the preceding generation, represented by the father, but also by the uncles and aunts bearing the same surname, and guardians for their part of the family honor and interests. Moreover, the fact that the mother had kept her own name often left open the possibility of recourse to the maternal side of the family. Not all families, even those of the aristocracy, made use of this possibility, but if they did, then the historian

---

[18]Céline Perol, "Sortir de l'anonymat: apparition et diffusion des noms de famille à Cortone, XIIIe–XVIe siècles," in *Genèse médiévale de l'anthroponymie moderne. L'espace italien,* ed. Menant and Martin (Rome, 1994), p. 568.

has only to identify what was the stock of family names used regularly in order to define the place of the individual in his lineage. In Portugal as in Tuscany it is the "familial name" which takes the place of the family name as surname. The latter only became dominant when people adopted a different anthroponymic logic.

THE FRENCH MIDI REFLECTED IN PERSONAL NAMES

Benoît Cursente

At the outset, I would like to call attention to the fact that I was provided with the substance of this paper by the work of the Azay-le-Ferron research group, to which I belong.[1] The question I would like to address is this: to what extent can we consider the medieval social organization of the French Midi revealed by personal names?

I wish to stress three methodological considerations that constitute the framework of my paper. The first is but a truism: we have to consider carefully to what extent disparity is due to the heterogeneity and the discontinuity of the source materials—ecclesiastical cartularies mainly—as well as their uneven utilization by modern scholars. Next, we have to define accurately the nature of the course of our demonstration. So, if we consider microregional realities only, we can easily prove that personal names studies merely reveal the anarchical juxtaposition of many kinship strategies. We are, in a way, faced with the issue raised by pointillist painting. That is, we have to wonder which is the appropriate distance for the eye to make out the meaningful units. In other words, how far away from the picture must the onlooker stand to distinguish the designs formed by the dots? If he or she steps back, would this alter the meaning of the images? Finally, we can reconstruct a different historical reality depending on

---

[1] *Genèse médiévale de l'anthroponymie moderne* (= GMAM). *I. Études d'anthroponymie médiévale Ie et IIe rencontres, Azay-le-Ferron 1986 et 1987*, ed. Monique Bourin (1990); GMAM, *II. Persistances du nom unique*, 1, *Le cas de la Bretagne. L'anthroponymie des clercs. 2, Désignation et anthroponymie des femmes. Méthodes statistiques pour l'anthroponymie*, ed. Monique Bourin and Pascal Chareille (1992); GMAM, *III. Enquêtes généalogiques et données prosopographiques*, ed. Monique Bourin and Pascal Chareille (1995); GMAM, *IV. Discours sur le nom: normes, usages, imaginaire (VIe–XVIe siècles)*, ed. Patrice Beck (1997).

whether we consider all the facts as a whole or only part of them. To use another visual metaphor, it may be useful to put the proper filter on the lens of the camera to make an aerial survey.

Identification of the Distinctive Personal Name Stock of the French Midi

Making use of names,[2] I shall endeavor to describe the Midi in its European context. At the present state of our knowledge, the French Midi appears on a medieval European map with somewhat blurred boundaries. On the one hand, Provence, and mainly its eastern part, appears to be a gradual transition between the Languedocian and Ligurian regions, though more closely related to the former.[3] On the other hand, the continuity between Languedoc and Catalonia now stands out more clearly.[4] In the western part, on both sides of the Pyrenees, in Gascony, Aragon, and Navarre, it is obvious that the personal namestock was characterized by common features until the end of the first millennium, as we shall see in greater detail later.

---

[2]Benoît Cursente, "Aspects de la 'révolution anthroponymique' dans le Midi de la France (début XIe–début XIIIe siècle)," in *L'anthroponymie. Document de l'histoire sociale des mondes méditerranéens médiévaux*, ed. Monique Bourin, Jean-Marie Martin, and François Menant, Collections de l'École française de Rome 226 (Rome, 1996), pp. 41–62.

[3]Alain Venturini, "Les noms de baptême de Nice et du pays niçois, XIIIe–XVe siècles," *Mémoires de l'Académie du Vaucluse* 6 (1985), 179–97; B. Z. Keddar, "Noms de saints et mentalités populaires à Gênes au XIVe siècle," *Le Moyen Age* 73 (1967), 431–46; Alain Birolini, "Étude d'anthroponymie génoise," *Mélanges de l'École française de Rome. Moyen âge* 107/2 (1995), 467–96.

[4]Michel Zimmermann, "Les débuts de la révolution anthroponymique en Catalogne (Xe–XIIe siècles)," in Charles Higounet, Pierre Bonnassie, and Jean-Bernard Marquette, eds., *Cadres de vie et société dans le Midi médiéval*, Annales du Midi 102 (Toulouse, 1990), pp. 289–308.; Lluís To Figueras, "Antroponimia de los condados catalanes (Barcelona, Girona y Osona siglos X–XII)," in *Antroponimia y sociedad. Sistemas de identificacion hispano-cristianos en los siglos IX a XIII*, ed. Pascual Martínez Sopena (Santiago de Compostela-Valladolid, 1995), 371–94.

In short, personal names confirm the close relationship between the medieval French Midi and the Iberian Peninsula, which is itself a plural entity. Compared with northern France, southern distinctiveness was undeniable. Between the two we can note the existence of a central France, which constitutes a wide and gradual transition.[5] The onomastic distinctiveness of the Midi lies, first and foremost, in the rapid and full triumph of the twofold name system as Monique Bourin has demonstrated. Around the year 1100, south of a line from Nantes to Lyons, more than half of the laymen designated in the charters bore twofold names. That sudden and sweeping change explains how we may speak of an "onomastic revolution" in the French Midi. In most regions, the twofold name system came after a transitional stage during which the *nomen proprium* was followed by an additional designation ("fils de," *qui dicitur).* In the Midi, people opted directly for the alternative of the *nomen paternum* (*Petrus Raimundi).* And finally, in the twelfth century, the *nomen paternum* came to be overtaken by the place name (*Petrus de Ponte).* From that broad generalization about the Midi, I will now try to come to a clearer view by dealing with one specific issue.

A Common Namestock for the Land of the Troubadours?

I need not stress that from the end of the eleventh century, a civilization characterized by the blossoming of a secular culture emerged in the Midi. This culture, dedicated to *"l'art d'aimer,"* was illustrated by the troubadours. Finally, in the thirteenth century, the Midi asserted itself as the country of the *lingua occitana* (or *"Occitania"*), and as the country of the "troubadours."[6] So, to what extent does this new personal naming

---

[5]Monique Bourin, "France du Midi et France du Nord: deux systèmes anthroponymiques?," in *L'anthroponymie. Document d'histoire sociale*, ed. Bourin et al., pp. 179–202.

[6]Linda M. Paterson, *The World of the Troubadours: Medieval Occitan Society, c. 1100–c. 1300* (Cambridge, 1993); Geneviève Brunel-Lobrichon and Claudie Duhamel-Amado, *Au temps des troubadours: XIIe–XIIIe siècles* (Paris, 1997).

system reflect the echo of the new occitanic culture? In an attempt to answer this question, I will put a special filter on my lens. In other words, I will consider one aspect only of anthroponomy, that is, the frequency of different baptismal names.

The classical expansion of the phenomenon of the troubadours was, as it is widely acknowledged, connected to a particular geography and sociology of powers, namely the lords' and princes' courts, most highly concentrated in the region between Toulouse and the Rhône Valley. Let us have a closer look at the evolution of baptismal names in that area. Between the second half of the eleventh century and the beginning of the twelfth, we notice a massive partiality for a few leading baptismal names. They accounted for from 65 to 85 percent of the total. This frequency constitutes what can be called an occitan onomastical unit.

I wish to emphasize the three following points. In the first place, this onomastical unit was characteristic of a vast area, which can be geographically delineated from the Atlantic Ocean to the Rhône Valley. In the second place, this leading group of names was composed of four "pan-occitan" names, and a fifth name limited to a single region. The names found throughout the entire region are *Petrus* (Peir), *Guillelmus* (Guillem), *Bernardus* (Bernat), and *Raimundus* (Raimon). The fifth one was *Pontius* (Pons) in the Languedoc, *Hugo* (Huc) in the Quercy, and *Arnaldus* (Arnaut) in the Gascony. Thirdly, these leading names remained surprisingly stable until the middle of the thirteenth century.[7]

One might be tempted to suspect a correlation between this onomastical area and the phenomenon of the troubadours. Two very convincing arguments may be put forward to assert that any relationship was pure coincidence between these two isolated features. The first argument lies in the fact that this group of names, already present in the cartulary of Agde around the middle of the eleventh century as Bourin has demonstrated, was established prior to, and *ipso facto* independent of, the

---

[7]Cursente, "Aspects de la 'revolution anthroponymique'."

appearance of the troubadours.[8] The second argument in support of this approach is, as Michael Mitterauer has brilliantly shown, that the increased preference for certain princely names was the result of the consolidation of vassalic and feudal powers between the prince and his subjects, leading to the creation of kinship bonds expressed by personal names.[9]

In spite of these arguments, it does not seem far-fetched to me to theorize that the troubadours nonetheless had some influence on the long-lived predominance of that "panoccitan" onomastical unit. The main reason for this assumption is the fact that the geographical extent of this practice extended beyond political and cultural boundaries for a long period of time. For instance, it was natural in the region of Bordeaux to place one's children under the invocation of *Guillem*, a ducal name *par excellence*. However, that reasoning does not explain the partiality enjoyed by the name of *Raimundus* (Raimon).[10] Needless to say, Raimon is the name of the Counts of Toulouse, the traditional rivals of the Dukes of Aquitania.

In a nutshell, the common symbolic heritage to which the people of Occitania referred when giving names did not obey a strictly political or vassalic logic. On balance, I am prone to think that, to some degree, the Occitan onomastical unit is the echo of the troubadours' *koine*, the common scripta of the medieval Midi. The troubadours, who moved from court to court, and from the service of one prince to another, must have contributed to spreading the idea that there was a heritage of common princely references over and above the former ethnic and dialectical diversities, and beyond the political rivalry of the times.

---

[8]Monique Bourin, "Les formes anthroponymiques et leur évolution d'après les données du cartulaire du chapitre cathédral d'Agde (Xe siècle–1250)," in GMAM I, ed. Bourin, pp. 179–217.

[9]Michael Mitterauer, *Ahnen und Heilige. Namengebung in der europäischen Geschichte* (Munich, 1993).

[10]See the *index nominum* of the *Grand Cartulaire de la Sauve Majeure*, ed. Charles Higounet, Arlette Higounet-Nadal, and Nicole de Peña (Bordeaux, 1996).

Identification of a Multiplicity of Socio-cultural Areas

By altering the scale of our analysis, we can make out a multiplicity of socio-cultural areas in the Midi. However, the different sets cannot be perceived with equal clarity. To illustrate the truth of this, four different cases can be contrasted, two-by-two.

Let us consider the first contrast. We notice, on the one hand, regions that show blurred characteristics because of the backward state of modern research. Such is the case with Provence or Auvergne. On the other hand, a region particularly well known thanks to the quality of recent research, is the lower Languedoc, studied by Bourin[11] and Claudie Duhamel-Amado.[12] As regards the second contrast, there are regions presenting blurred characteristics due to their position as transitional areas between the north and the south (as in the case of Limousin) that are to be set alongside a region that stands out because of its marginal location; here I refer to Gascony. I wish to focus our attention on the two cases that can be better observed, namely Languedoc and Gascony.

Given that the Azay-le-Ferron team started its investigation after Bourin had advanced her hypothesis about Languedoc, it is not surprising that this region should exemplify the so-called "anthroponymical revolution" of the eleventh and twelfth centuries. The findings of our group on this subject are already well known. Languedoc holds a central position in personal names studies for still another reason. It is the region where studies on personal names, kinship, and social history in general have been most highly integrated.

This results mainly from Duhamel-Amado's thesis, which is soon to be published. I confine myself to two points in her important doctoral thesis. The first point is the moment in social history when the new system

---

[11]Bourin, refer to notes 1, 5, and 8.

[12]Claudie Duhamel-Amado, "La famille aristocratique languedocienne. Parenté, patrimoine dans les vicomtés de Béziers et Agde (900–1170)" (Ph.D. diss., Université de Paris IV, 1994).

of naming with two elements was first set up. Contrary to what one might think, that watershed was not prior to 1050; that is the time when the parental group identified itself with a territory focused on a castle (*castrum*). It dates from the next generation only, when the old traditional kinship structure, a cognatic network of cousins, gave way to a vertical and agnatic structure. The ancestor to whom the system referred was the founder of the lineage, and not the founder of the *castrum*. A single, but striking example of this trend is that we find that Guido, founder of the castrum of Aumelas, was also the first of the Lords of Montpellier. Paradoxically, until the thirteenth century, these lords would continue to refer to Guillem, son of Guido, as founder of the lineage. In the second half of the eleventh century, the adoption of the *nomen paternum* system, such as in the name *Petrus Raimundi*, is a phase of transition during which a more restricted family unit identified itself with a territorial power. And after the eleventh century, the reference to a place name like *Petrus de Villanova* was linked to the triumph of a kinship structure that had to cut off the secondary branches. Duhamel-Amado also broadens our knowledge of the popularization of princely names among the aristocratic kingroups. The unusual names of the earlier namestock thrived best among the secondary lineages edged out by the latter structure. Conversely, adopting a widespread name was equivalent to claiming rights to the main lordship.

Finally, I wish to focus attention on Gascony, which I know more precisely because of my own personal research. Three main facts are typical of the medieval Gascon personal naming system. First, until 1000, that region was distinct from the Midi, and was in complete harmony with the Basco-Navarrese side of the Pyrenees.[13] This amounts to saying that the two regions shared the same stock of popular names (*Garsia,*

---

[13]Benoît Cursente, "Étude sur les formes anthroponymiques dans les cartulaires du chapitre métropolitain de Sainte-Marie d'Auch (XIe–XIIIes)," in GMAM I, pp. 143–78, and "Aspects de la 'révolution anthroponymique'"; Angeles Libano Zumulacarregui and Jose Angel Libano, "La antroponimia en Alava, Guipuzcoa y Vizcaya en los siglos X a XIII," in *Antroponimia y sociedad*, ed. Martínez Sopena, pp. 259–96; J.-A. Garcia de Cortàzar, "Antroponomia en Navarra y Rioja en los siglos XI y XII," ibid., pp. 297–326.

Sancho, Aznar, Lop) and the use of a two-fold designation system (a *nomen paternum* like *Garsia Sanchez*), whereas elsewhere the *nomen proprium* alone prevailed. The anthroponimic analysis shows clearly that around the middle of the eleventh century this province was won over to the practices of the French side, in very short order, and for good. This change was marked in two ways: first, with the appearance of Germanic names (*Raimon, Guillem, Bernad, Arnaut, Otto*), and second with the addition of the place name to the first name, like *Arnaut de Agromont*, or to the *nomen paternum*, like *Guilem Ramon de Agromont*. Finally, during the twelfth and thirteenth centuries, the Gascon naming system acquired many of the peculiarities of the French Midi. I will underline only two of them related to the position of women.[14]

More often than not, women were designated by a single *nomen proprium*. Yet, in the heart of Gascony, when married women intervene as principals in a charter, at least half of them were designated by a two-fold name; for instance, *Comdor de Lafitte*, a first name and a surname. To put this percentage in perspective, one need only note that five percent of women were so named in documents from lower Languedoc. Generally, married women were designated by names indicating their membership in their husbands' families. However, in Gascony, up to 86 percent of the married women continued to be referred to by their parental names.

Conclusion

In the Midi as elsewhere, names were the expression of personal identity, whether shown in an active or passive way, by which I mean consciously or unconsciously. When names represent the autonomous construction of a family unit, they manifest a structure that can only be understood through an intimate knowledge of kinship structures and family strategies. Since that knowledge is scarcely attainable through the

---

[14]Benoît Cursente, "Les femmes de Gascogne et leur nom d'après le cartulaire de Berdoues (milieu XIIe–milieu XIIIe siècle)," in GMAM II.2, pp. 111–32.

study of cartularies, we can set a question mark against the frequency of that case. For the most part, names seem to stand more or less consciously for processes of adhesion or identification. They echo the multiple influences that are exercised on the family unit itself at the core of meaningful choices: identification with the ruling king or lord, cohesion to a wider ethnic or cultural community, expression of belonging to the Christian community. And finally, the importance of these different aspects depends on the differing perspectives of the historians who study them.

WHAT WERE PEOPLE CALLED IN COMMUNAL ITALY?

François Menant

This paper presents a synthesis of the results obtained by a group of Italian, French, German, and Austrian historians, who, from 1990 to 1997, studied the evolution of the naming system of northern and central Italy from the time of the single name (during the High Middle Ages) to the time of the modern two-name system.[1] This research group used the method that proved efficient in France in the program *Genèse médiévale de l'anthroponymie moderne*,[2] and adapted it to the peculiarities of the Italian situation.[3] The documentary basis consists in large archival collections, and lists of citizens or taxpayers. The main stage of the inquiry was a dozen or so case studies of cities and small regions scattered through northern and central Italy, and as far as possible, representative cultural areas such as Tuscany, Rome, or the great cities of the north.[4] I must stress

---

[1]Published as *Genèse médiévale de l'anthroponymie moderne. L'espace italien* in *Mélanges de l'École française de Rome. Moyen Âge* [= MEFRM] 106/2 (1994), 107/2 (1995), and 110/1 (1998); *L'anthroponymie. Document de l'histoire sociale des mondes méditerranéens médiévaux*, ed. Monique Bourin, Jean-Marie Martin, and François Menant (Rome, 1996).

[2]*Genèse médiévale de l'anthroponymie moderne. Études d'anthroponymie médiévale.* 4 vols. in 5 parts (Tours, 1989–97).

[3]See the introductions of Martin and Menant to the MEFRM volumes *Genèse médiévale de l'anthroponymie moderne: L'espace italien.*

[4]Chieri (Mirella Montanari), Genova (Alain Birolini), Milan (Patrizia Corrarati), Piacenza (Pierre Racine), Reggio Emilia (Olivier Guyotjeannin), Pisa (Enrica Salvatori), San Salvatore a Isola (Siena; Maria Ginatempo), Cortona (Céline Perol), Rome (Étienne Hubert and Tommaso di Carpegna Falconieri), all issued in MEFRM, *L'espace italien* 1 (106/2) and 2 (107/2).

the point that this research is not mainly a linguistic one, for we have little competency in that field. Its purpose is to enhance, from a distinctive point of view, our knowledge of Italian society in the age of communes. In our minds, the evolution of the naming system reflects that of a society, and helps us to understand it. I shall develop three points in my paper: the naming system, the choice of personal names, and finally, some distinctive features of Italian society as factors in the evolution of naming.

The Personal Name System: Italian Traits and Inner Diversities

As regards the naming system, the evolution shown by our mono-graphic studies is, in its main components, similar to that of France, Spain,[5] and southern Italy.[6] At the beginning of the eleventh century, the single name still predominated, alone or accompanied by other elements that were not yet stable parts of it. A usual designation was, for instance, *Tedaldus filius quondam Alberti de loco Ronco*. Later on, those complementary elements were more and more often regularly included in the name: for example, *Albertus Dominici, Petrus de Puteo*, or nicknames like *Iohannes Russus*, or *Bernardus Mazabovem*. This second element, which characterized the new naming system, would sooner or later become the hereditary sur-name. Most of the time it referred to the family, above all as a *nomen paternum*. Place names and nicknames were the two other main origins of Italian surnames, while occupational names were only popular among the urban population.

As regards the chronology of this evolution, it was more or less the same in Italy as in the other countries, but the movement was slower and more hesitant than in France or Spain. Two-element names became stand-

---

[5]*Antroponimia y sociedad. Sistemas de identificación hispano-cristianos en los siglos IX a XIII*, ed. Pascual Martínez Sopena (Santiago de Compostela-Valladolid, 1995).

[6]See various papers in MEFRM, *L'espace italien*, and Jean-Marie Martin, "L'Italie méri-dionale," in *L'anthroponymie. Document de l'histoire sociale*, ed. Bourin et al., pp. 29–39.

ard before the end of the eleventh century in Rome,[7] but only during the twelfth century in most northern cities, around 1250 in Pisa,[8] and not until the seventeenth century in other places in Tuscany.[9] These remarks are only valid for masculine names; as elsewhere in Europe,[10] women usually bore a single name, completed by their father's or their husband's name.

Italian anthroponomy presents an important peculiarity, which had lasting consequences: whereas in most European countries the evolution stopped when the two-element name became dominant, in Italy it continued for a long period, and in many regions the surname did not become hereditary before the end of the Middle Ages.[11] Venice was in fact the only place where the surname, which here was nearly always a *nomen paternum*, was fixed and in most cases definitively and without further evolution, as early as the ninth century.[12] It is noticeable that Venice shared in that way

[7]Étienne Hubert, "Evolution générale de l'anthroponymie masculine à Rome du Xe au XIIIe siècle," in *L'espace italien* 1 [MEFRM, 106/2 (1994)], pp. 573–94.

[8]Enrica Salvatori, "Il sistema antroponimico a Pisa nel Duecento: la città e il territorio," in *L'espace italien* 2 [MEFRM, 107/2 (1995)], pp. 427–66.

[9]Céline Perol, "Sortir de l'anonymat: apparition et diffusion des noms de famille à Cortone, XIIIe–XVIe siècle," in *L'espace italien* 1 [MEFRM 106/2 (1994)], pp. 559–71; Christiane Klapisch-Zuber, "Les faux-semblants de l'identité. Noms de lignée, noms cachés, noms-refuges à Florence au XIVe siècle," in *L'espace italien* 3 [MEFRM 110/1 (1998)], pp. 159–72; Anthony Molho, "Noms, mémoire, identité publique à Florence à la fin du Moyen Age," ibid., pp. 137–57. See also Philippe Jansen, "L'anthroponymie dans les Marches du milieu du XIIIe siècle à la fin du XVe siècle: archaïsme ou régression?," ibid., pp. 201–25; Giacomo Casarino, "Alla ricerca di 'nome e parentado': Genova e distretto tra Quattro e Cinquecento," ibid., pp. 227–45.

[10]GMAM, *II. Persistances du nom unique. 2, Désignation et anthroponymie des femmes. Méthodes statistiques pour l'anthroponymie*, ed. Monique Bourin and Pascal Chareille (1992). The greater part of this volume is dedicated to the surnames of the women.

[11]See *L'espace italien* 3 [MEFRM 110/1 (1998)]: the whole volume is dedicated to that problem.

[12]Gianfranco Folena, "Gli antichi nomi di persona e la storia civile di Venezia," in *Atti e Memorie dell'Istituto Veneto di Scienze, Lettere ed Arti, Classe di Scienze Morali, Lettere ed*

the situation of other Byzantine spheres of influence like Bari or Naples,[13] and to a lesser degree, Rome.[14] But the Venetian situation was unique in northern Italy. Tuscany offered the opposite pattern, with a very slow evolution toward stable and hereditary *cognomina*: in the Florentine *catasto* of 1427, only 16 percent of the families had such a stable name; all the others were identified by the names of their father and grandfather, as *Lapo di Giovanni di Antonio*.[15] In other regions, the evolution pointed towards the victory of the two-element name, but only after a long period of transition. During several generations, a large percentage of individuals, up to 25 percent of the whole, bore nicknames or second names introduced by a formula like *qui vocatur* or *qui dicitur*; for example, *Albertus qui vocatur de Puteo*. In Rome, Milan, or Reggio Emilia, that transitional period covers the whole eleventh century.

The lasting complexity and instability of the name system was probably a general feature of most Italian regions in the late Middle Ages, as some recent studies have shown, especially in Emilian towns such as Bologna and Parma. A good example is given by the lists of members of the city council of Parma during the thirteenth and fourteenth centuries: some of them bore rather classical two-element names, with a forename and a surname, others *nomina paterna*, while many others bore chains of

---

Arti 129 (1970–71), 445–84, and *Culture e lingue nel Veneto medievale* (Padua, 1990), pp. 175–210.

[13]Jean-Marie Martin, "Anthroponymie et onomastique à Bari (950–1250)," in *L'espace italien* 1 [MEFRM 106/2 (1994)], pp. 683–701; Matteo Villani, "L'antroponimia nelle carte napoletane (secc. X–XIII)," in *L'espace italien* 2 [MEFRM 107/2 (1995)], pp. 345–59; Errico Cuozzo, "Qualche nota sul'antroponimia aristocratica di Gaeta tra IX e XI secolo," ibid., pp. 343–44; Cuozzo, "L'antroponimia aristocratica nel *Regnum Siciliae*. L'esempio dell'Abruzzo nel Catalogus baronum (1150–1168)," in *L'espace italien* 1 [MEFRM 106/2 (1994)], pp. 654–56.

[14]Hubert, "Evolution générale."

[15]David Herlihy and Christiane Klapisch-Zuber, *Les Toscans et leurs familles: une étude du "catasto" florentin de 1427* (Paris, 1978), pp. 532–43.

personal names in Florentine style, or a collective name such as *de Barateriis* or *de Rossis*. Those systems were often combined, giving way to rather complicated designations. A relative of the chronicler Salimbene de Adam was called *Bernardinus Oliverii Rolandi Oliverii*, and the jurist Odofredus *dominus Odofredus doctor legum filius quondam domini Bonacursii Ricardi de Denariis*, while another Bolognese bore the name of *Guido Cazanimici Alberti Ursi de Cazanimicis*.[16] In fact the predominant pattern seems to have been a complex system based on references to a main household, and to as many ancestors as necessary to allow the identification of the person in urban society. That structure of names corresponded in fact to a political and social organization that was in great part based on patrician households. Once again, the best examples of such a situation are to be found in Tuscany and especially in Florence, where they have been analyzed by Christiane Klapisch-Zuber.[17]

Another aspect of the variability of the system is that an individual may be designated in more or less sophisticated ways, according to the documents. Concern with complex systems was to be found above all in the leading groups, the urban aristocracy, but it is clear that such rising classes as the merchants and craftsmen of the *popolo* adopted that fashion as part of their acculturation to the aristocratic way of life. One should not believe, however, that those trends were absolutely standard in the Italy of the communes: I have myself recently studied the case of the city of Cremona, and found that around 1300 most of the inhabitants, of whatever social standing, were designated, in a very simple modern way,

---

[16]Olivier Guyotjeannin, "L'onomastique émilienne (XIe–milieu XIIIe siècle). Le cas de Reggio Emilia d'après le fonds de San Prospero," in *L'espace italien* 1 [MEFRM 106/2 (1994)], pp. 381–446.

[17]Christiane Klapisch-Zuber, "Les faux-semblants"; see also the papers collected in the two volumes by Klapisch-Zuber: *La maison et le nom. Stratégies et rituels dans l'Italie de la Renaissance* (Paris, 1990); and *Women, Family, and Ritual in Renaissance Italy*, trans. Lydia Cochrane (Chicago, 1985).

by a forename and a surname that appears to have been hereditary.[18] This example confirms the fact that communal Italy was a world of variety, and that only exhaustive, but absolutely impossible research, could allow us to establish general laws of evolution. In the present state of research, we can only point to general tendencies, nothing more.

Personally, I think that social differences are still more important than local ones. For instance, while the leading urban classes developed sophisticated systems of identification,[19] many peasants of the Quattrocento and even citizens of a small town like Cortona, in Tuscany,[20] had not yet acquired a stable surname. The classical analysis of the Florentine *catasto* by Klapisch-Zuber and David Herlihy shows very well a fact that can be confirmed by other, less rich, sources. The sophistication and the stability of the naming system were linked with two main factors: a person's position in the social scale, as determined by his wealth and political influence, and his distance from the city. A member of a patrician family of Florence or Parma had three or four names, which taken together placed him clearly in the hierarchy of urban wealth and power. On the other hand, the poorest peasants and serfs may have had only one name (sometimes down to the seventeenth century), to which they added a commonplace nickname or their father's name when the fiscal or seigneurial clerks asked for a more precise identification. A source like the *Liber paradisus*,

---

[18]François Menant, "Comment s'appelaient les habitants de Crémone vers 1300? Contribution à l'histoire du nom de famille en Italie," in *L'espace italien* 3 [MEFRM 110/1 (1998)], pp. 183–200.

[19]Olivier Guyotjeannin, "Problèmes de la dévolution du nom et du surnom dans les élites d'Italie centroseptentrionale," in *L'espace italien* 2 [MEFRM 107/2 (1995)], pp. 556–94; Nikolai Wandruszka, "Die Entstehung des Familiennamens in Bologna (XII. und XIII. Jahrhundert)," ibid., pp. 595–625; François Menant, "Ancêtres et patrimoine. Les systèmes de désignation dans l'aristocratie lombarde des XIe–XIIe siècles" in *Nomen et gens. Zur historischen Aussagekraft frühmittelalterlicher Personennamen*, ed. Dieter Geuenich, Wolfgang Haubrichs, and Jörg Jarnut (Berlin, 1997), pp. 176–89.

[20]Perol, "Sortir de l'anonymat."

the list of the serfs of the Bolognese district in 1257, confirms the difference existing between the complex names of the lords, referring to social connections and long series of ancestors, and those of their serfs, reduced to elementary forms.[21]

Another example pointing to an analogous conclusion is that of the village of Aspra, not very far from Rome: a close analysis shows that the *cognomen* became standard there four or five generations later than in the neighboring great town.[22] We find the same backwardness in the evolution if we observe the choice of the Christian names. From lists of inhabitants of Roquebrune, on the Genoese Riviera, Benjamin Z. Kedar noticed that the people living in that village bore the same forenames as the Genoese who lived a hundred years earlier;[23] in Florence, the name *Martinus*, once very widespread, became insulting after the middle of the thirteenth century. After that time it was still borne by many peasants, but no longer by the citizens, who preferred more modern names like *Filippo* or *Giacomo*.[24] If we further analyze those differences and variations in naming evolution, we notice that, in fact, in the Italian society of the communal era several systems of designation co-existed and influenced one another. The old seigneurial aristocracy of the deeply feudalized Po plain, for instance, took

[21]François Menant, "Une source pour l'étude de l'anthroponymie servile: le *Liber Paradisus* (Bologne, 1257)," to be published in GMAM VI; see also Menant, "L'anthroponymie du monde rural," in *L'anthroponymie. Document de l'histoire sociale*, ed. Bourin et al., pp. 349–63.

[22]Étienne Hubert, "Structures urbaines et système anthroponymique (A propos de l'Italie centro-septentrionale, Xe–XIIIe siècle)," in *L'anthroponymie. Document de l'histoire sociale*, ed. Bourin et al., pp. 313–47.

[23]Benjamin Z. Kedar, "Noms de saints et mentalité populaire à Gênes, au XIVe siècle," *Le Moyen Age* 73 (1967), 431–46.

[24]Olof Brattö, *Studi di antroponimia fiorentina. Il libro di Montaperti (an. MCCLX)* (Göteborg, 1953), pp. 33–35; compare Gianfranco Folena, "Fra i Lapi e i Bindi del Duecento: note di antroponimia fiorentina," in *Culture e lingue nel Veneto Medievale*, ed. Folena (Padua, 1990), pp. 211–26.

the names of their castles in accordance with the use of many other European aristocratic families, and sometimes added a collective title taken from the feudal hierarchy such as *capitanei de Raude, confanonerii de Cicognara* or *seniores de Rodengo*. On the other hand, the urban élites mostly bore the name of an ancestor, and when a branch withdrew from the household it took the name of its founder.[25] As we have seen, this system was to predominate from the thirteenth century onwards, with the generalization of names like *Alberti* or *de Albertis*. At a lower level of urban society, small merchants and craftsmen usually bore only two names, the second one being often a nickname or an occupational name such as *Ferrarius* or *Textor*. At the bottom of the social ladder, poor peasants often lacked even a surname. Those various designation systems were far from being unchangeable. The main tendency among the rich was to adopt a complex eponymous designation system based on the model of the urban patriciate. But every group in the complex society of communal Italy displayed its own designation system, which reflected its material and cultural wealth, its links with political power, its proximity to the town, and, finally, its collective self-awareness.

Personal Names

My second point will deal with the choice of personal names.[26] I prefer to say personal names rather than forenames or Christian names, at least until the thirteenth century, because, as we shall see, many people

---

[25]Menant, "Ancêtres et patrimoine"; and "Les modes de dénomination de l'aristocratie italienne aux XIe et XIIe siècles: premières réflexions à partir d'exemples lombards," in *L'espace italien* 2 [MEFRM 107/2 (1995)], pp. 535–55.

[26]I shall use information collected in the papers mentioned above, especially in MEFRM, *L'espace italien*. See also Elizabeth Carpenter, "Les prénoms à Orvieto à la fin du XIIIe siècle," in *Villes, bonnes villes, cités et capitales: Études d'histoire urbaine (XII–XVIII siècle) offertes à Bernard Chevalier*, ed. Monique Bourin (Tours, 1989), pp. 371–79; and Alberto Grohmann, *L'imposizione diretta nei comuni dell'Italia centrale nel XIII secolo. La libra di Perugia del 1285* (Perugia-Rome, 1986), esp. pp. 107–08, 121–27, 142–45.

bore only one name, and that single name very often had no link with a saint or any other Christian reference. As for the choice of personal names, Italy shared roughly the evolution of the other western countries, which was characterized by several concomitant phenomena: Christian names became more popular, and German names regressed, but they did so very slowly in northern Italy, where Lombard and Frankish onomastics remained very widespread. The main evolution, at least quantitatively, was the concentration on the choices of a few names, borne by an ever larger part of the population: above all *John*, followed by *Peter* and *James*.

The main characteristic of Italian names of that period, however, was their extreme individualization. Many names were derivatives of an existing name, and many more were creations of new names. For instance, the first method created the very common Florentine names *Bindo* and *Lapo* as diminutives of *Jacobus* and *Aldobrandus*,[27] or *Guidottus* and *Johanninus* from *Guido* and *Johannes*. By adding a qualifying adjective, one got the very usual *Iohannnesbonus* (*Zambonus*) and *Ottobonus*. The most popular names, such as *Johannes, Ugo*, or *Guido*, had a lot of those diminutives and derivatives, which could be used more than the original name. For instance, in Pisa in 1228, *Ugolino* was eight times more frequent than *Ugo*.

Moreover, there was an extraordinarily high number of rare or unique names, which were borne only by one or by few people in one city. Twenty-eight percent of the Florentine soldiers bore such names in 1260.[28] Some of those very unique names express for example a wish, as *Detesalvus* or *Omnibene*; others are nicknames borne as single names or forenames. Nobles, for instance, were fond of warlike names as *Salinguerra, Vinciguerra*, or *Vincicastello*, and many ordinary people were called *Mangiavacca, Russus, Bracciaforte, Mezovillano*, or even *Senzanome*. In twelfth-century northern Italy, we found a series of scatological names like *Cagainputeo*,

---

[27]Brattö, *Studi di antroponimia fiorentina*; Folena, "Fra i Lapi."

[28]Olof Brattö, *Nuovi studi di antroponimia fiorentina. I nomi meno frequenti del Libro di Montaperti (An. MCCLX)* (Stockholm, 1955).

"defecates in the oven," or *Cagainbraga*, "defecates in his trousers." The name of the family could be used as a forename too, and many nobles are called *Amatus de Amatis* or *Ponzonus de Ponzonibus*.

As a consequence of those tendencies, the population of the period of the communes was split between a large number of people bearing a few very common names, and many others who had hundreds of very rare names. In Rome for example, between 1100 and 1250, about one-third of the men were called *Peter* or *John*, while 50 percent bore a rare or very rare name.[29]

In the last decades of the thirteenth century a new change took place, as a result of which forenames became much more modern, by which I mean closer to our own taste. In fact the mass of diminutives and nicknames, which had made so strange the landscape of Italian names, disappeared and gave way to names of saints, especially great saints. Kedar noticed, for example, that among the consuls and other rulers of Genoa, only 12 percent bore saints' names in the twelfth century, but 25 percent did in the thirteenth century, and more than 50 percent did so in the fourteenth century.[30] That change was studied above all in Tuscany and Umbria; de La Roncière and Herlihy showed, from detailed studies of the Florentine population, that it took place more precisely between 1280 and 1320 or 1340.[31] In the *catasto* of Orvieto of 1292, most of the men were already called by "new" names such as *Dominicus, Franciscus, Mattheus, Angelo, Andrea*, besides such traditional names as *John, Peter*, and *James*.

---

[29]Hubert, "Evolution générale."

[30]Kedar, "Noms de saints."

[31]Charles-M. de La Roncière, "L'influence des Franciscains dans la campagne de Florence au XIVe siècle (1280–1360)," *Mélanges de l'Ecole française de Rome. Moyen Age, Temps modernes* 87 (1975), pp. 27–103. Italian translation in Charles-M. de La Roncière, ed., *Tra preghiera e rivolta. Le folle toscane nel XIV secolo* (Rome, 1993), pp. 137–94. Also see de La Roncière's "Orientations pastorales du clergé, fin XIIIe–XIVe siècle: le témoignage de l'onomastique toscane," *Comptes-rendus de l'Académie des Inscriptions et Belles-Lettres* (1983), 43–64; David Herlihy, "Tuscan Names, 1200–1530," *Renaissance Quarterly* (1988), 561–82.

In other places we find *Antonius, Bartolomaeus, Laurentius,* and *Stefanus,* all names that sound very modern to our ears.[32] As a consequence, the total number of different names was reduced drastically: in Pistoia, fewer than 3 men bore the same name in 1219, but 4.4 did so in 1427. We can say that if many Italians of the Quattrocento were still very far from the modern system of denomination, on the other hand, the forenames they bore were also not so different from those current today.

Some Factors Influencing the Naming System in Central and Northern Italy

To conclude, I would like to point to two factors that may contribute to explaining the peculiarities of the Italian naming system in the age of the communes. The first is the presence of the notary, an essential character in the evolution of names.[33] His documents reflected all the aspects of everyday life, and when writing them he managed to follow the changing patterns of the verbal designations of people. But, inevitably, he had to translate the oral use into written formulas that were not exactly those of everyday use, and could not have its flexibility. Those written documents are today the unique source upon which we can rely to know the ways people used to refer to one another, and they express in fact the compromise between the "real" designation habits and their adaptation by the specialist of writing.[34]

Another decisive factor in the evolution of naming is communal organization itself. It represents, in fact, the Italian version of the state that developed everywhere in western countries during that period, which exerted heavy pressure to fix in written documents the names of subjects,

---

[32]Carpentier, "Les prénoms à Orvieto."

[33]Guyotjeannin, "L'onomastique émilienne."

[34]About the "real" designation and its transcription, see Menant, "L'anthroponymie du monde rural."

of taxpayers, and of suspects. The commune presented however some peculiarities in comparison with monarchic or seigneurial states. Its subjects, or at least some of them, exercised power collectively themselves, and they were therefore enumerated, by hundreds and thousands, in many lists of members of the counsels of the city-state, soldiers, or citizens who approved treaties with other cities.[35] On the other hand, the precocity of administrative techniques in the communes, and the presence of numerous notaries and clerks in their offices, led to the production of abundant written sources, in which individuals were identified as precisely as possible. Among those documents, the fiscal ones, *estimi* and later *catasti*, were the most remarkable, and the most important for the social history of the uses of naming.[36] For instance, they played a great, and often decisive, part in the spreading of complex names among the peasantry. The fiscal lists forced peasants to write down a surname, while everyday practice seemed to remain much more hesitant. Finally, the intense and changing political life of the city-states gave a real importance to the precise identification of individuals and communities such as families, seigneurial groups, or neighbors. I have mentioned that the transformations of the names of the patrician households were partly due to political circumstances, being linked to their place in the urban community.[37] The problem of the name is at the very heart of the genesis of the modern state in Italy at the time of the communes and of the urban seigneuries, and it is in those arenas, the social and political, that the cultural identity of this country is most clearly shown.

I thank Professor George Beech and Mrs. Andrée Cabillic for their help in the translation of this paper from the French.

[35]The best study of such a list is that of Enrica Salvatori, *La popolazione pisana nel Duecento. Il patto di alleanza di Pisa con Siena, Pistoia e Poggibonsi del 1228* (Pisa, 1994), pp. 129–35. See also Salvatori's "Il sistema antroponimico."

[36]See, for example, Grohmann, *L'imposizione diretta.*

[37]On that theme, see especially the works of Klapisch-Zuber, mentioned above.

Personal Names and Family Structure in Medieval Southern Italy and Sicily

Jean-Marie Martin

The group that began at the end of 1991 to study the anthroponomy of medieval southern Italy and Sicily included eight persons; some worked on Sicily (Maria Luisa Gangemi, Iris Mirazita, Enrico Pispisa, Carmela Maria Rugolo), the others on continental southern Italy (Errico Cuozzo, André Jacob, Jean-Marie Martin, Matteo Villani).[1] A scholar from outside

---

[1] This group has taken part in three colloquia (Rome, 1993; Milan, 1994; Rome, 1997). The proceedings of the meetings have been published in the series *Mélanges de l'Ecole française de Rome. Moyen âge* (= MEFRM). The following is a list of the contributions, beginning with vol. 106, pub. 1994: Matteo Villani, "L'onomastica femminile nel ducato di Napoli: l'esempio di Maria"; Errico Cuozzo, "L'antroponimia aristocratica nel *Regnum Siciliae*. L'esempio dell'Abruzzo nel *Catalogus baronum* (1150–1168)"; Villani, "La genesi dell'antroponimia moderna in Capitanata: l'esempio di Troia (1034–1250)"; Jean-Marie Martin, "Anthroponymie et onomastique à Bari (950–1250)"; Carmela Maria Rugolo, "I documenti dell'area peloritana"; Iris Mirazita, "Gli atti di Agrigento e Palermo." Vol. 107, pub. 1995: Martin, "Anthroponymie de l'Italie méridionale lombarde (VIIIe–IXe siécles)"; Cuozzo, "Qualche nota sull'antroponimia aristocratica di Gaeta tra IX e XI secolo"; Villani, "L'antroponimia nelle carte napoletane (secc. X–XII)"; André Jacob, "L'anthroponymie greque du Salento méridional"; Rugolo, "L'antroponimia nelle carte latine di alcune abbazie calabresi nei secoli XI–XIII"; Maria Luisa Gangemi, "L'evoluzione antroponimica a Catania e Paternò attraverso le pergamene di San Nicolò l'Arena"; Mirazita, "L'antroponimia nelle imbreviature del notaio Adamo de Citella (1° registro: 1286–87)." Vol. 110, pub. 1998: Enrico Pispisa, "Coscienza familiare ed egemonia urbana: *milites, meliores* e *populares* a Messina fra XII e XIV secolo"; Mirazita, "Trasmissione del cognome nell'aristocrazia urbana e nell'aristocrazia del denaro a Palermo fra XIII e XIV secolo"; Martin, "Le devenir du *cognomen* et le début de l'émergence du nom de famille. Bari, 1266–1343"; Villani, "L'antroponimia rurale nei registri cavensi (sec. XIII–XIV)." Moreover, I have presented a summary of the results of the first two meetings: "L'Italie méridionale," in *L'anthroponymie. Document de l'histoire sociale des mondes méditeranéens*

the group, Annliese Nef, presented a specific study on the lists of Arab *villeins* of Norman Sicily from the end of the eleventh to the second half of the twelfth century;[2] but as this type of document is very different from the others and the results cannot easily be compared with ours, we shall not take it into account in the present paper.

The main characteristic of medieval southern Italy and Sicily is their division into many small cultural areas with different populations using different laws (Roman, Byzantine, Lombard), different languages (Latin, Greek, Arab), and belonging to different religions and denominations (Islam, Roman Catholicism, Greek Orthodoxy). The first political upheaval happened with the Lombard invasion of the sixth and seventh centuries, which divided the conquered regions from those that remained under imperial rule (Gaeta, Naples, Amalfi, southern Apulia, and southern Calabria). In addition, between the seventh and the ninth centuries, the latter two regions were largely populated by Greeks, who probably came from eastern Sicily; the island itself was occupied by Muslims in the ninth century.

At the end of the ninth century, Byzantium conquered Lombard Apulia, which took the name of "theme of Langobardia" and became an imperial military province of Latin language, of Roman rite, and of Lombard law. Finally Norman knights conquered southern Italy and Sicily between 1030 and 1091; in 1130 Roger II, count of Sicily and duke of Apulia, became the first king of Sicily.

Except, it is likely, for the Muslims, the overall family structure was the same among the different peoples: since at least Late Antiquity, the basic group was the two-generation family grounded on legal marriage, even if marriage was celebrated in different ways according to each people's

---

médiévaux, ed. Monique Bourin, Jean-Marie Martin, and François Menant (Rome, 1996), pp. 29–39.

[2]Annliese Nef, "Anthroponymie et jarâ'id de Sicile; une approche renouvelée de la structure sociale des communautés arabo-musulmanes de l'île sous les Normands," in *L'anthroponymie. Document de l'histoire sociale*, ed. Bourin et al., pp. 123–42.

specific law. Probably only the Greeks married in church prior to the twelfth century, when Roger II imposed religious marriage on all his subjects. But the composition and importance of the wife's wealth was not the same: the Lombard woman was under the legal authority of a *mundoald* all her life long, and she was the owner of a quarter of her husband's wealth (*Morgengabe*) while the Roman or Greek woman could act on her own. The Greek woman, when she married, received from her husband *hypobolon* and *theoretron*. The division of the inheritance was equal for all the children in the Roman and Byzantine regions, whereas the sons were advantaged in the Lombard lands.[3] But, generally speaking, the family structure was not deeply affected by such peculiarities and its evolution was very slow.

In another way there could exist a solidarity of some nuclear families of common origin, forming a purely theoretical large family; as everywhere, such a tendency seems to have been stronger among the members of aristocracy.[4] But in southern Italy and Sicily the boundaries of aristocracy were not clear at all, since aristocratic groups of various origins lived under Norman rule.[5] The official feudal aristocracy itself, tightly controlled by the monarchy, was composite, as it included Norman immigrants and Lombards, often linked together by marriage, and even some Greeks at the level of simple knights. But local groups of pre-Norman aristocrats still considered themselves as such, sometimes without entering the official feudal class. If the Neapolitan nobles and knights were rapidly assimilated

[3]Jean-Marie Martin, "La Pouille du VIe au XIIe siècle," *Collection de l'École française de Rome* 179 (1993), 532–62, and "Pratiques successorales en Italie méridionale (Xe–XIIe siècle): Romains, Grecs et Lombards," in *La transmission du patrimoine: Byzance et l'aire méditerranéenne*, ed. Joëlle Beaucamp and Gilbert Dagron (Paris, 1998), pp. 189–210.

[4]See Errico Cuozzo, *Catalogus baronum. Commentario*, Fonti per la Storia d'Italia 101 (Rome, 1984).

[5]Jean-Marie Martin, "Aristocraties et seigneuries en Italie méridionale aux XIe et XIIe siècles: essai de typologie," *Journal des Savants* (1999), 227–59.

into it, even though often retaining a distinctive status,[6] most of the old families of Amalfitan *comites* remained outside the feudal group until the Angevin period. The Lombard notables of many cities such as Bari did likewise, as did the Muslim *qâ'ids* of the royal court of Palermo.[7] Perhaps because their nobility was not official, the Amalfitans adopted a specific type of denomination: they were accustomed to list, after their personal name, the names of all their ancestors (father, grandfather, and so on) up to the first-known member of the dynasty, who generally had lived in the ninth or tenth century. So by the thirteenth century some names were followed by more than ten ancestors' names; this particular anthroponomy of the Amalfitan nobility "*dalla memoria lunga*" was studied by Mario Del Treppo.[8] So it is evident that the factors of ethnic and social differentiation were numerous.

Most of the anthroponymic studies of our group dealt with the period 950–1250 and tried to observe, as had been done already in France and in northern Italy, the rhythm of the spread, then the dominance, of the double denomination (name and surname). One only dealt with the eighth and ninth centuries, and the last contributions aimed to assess the establishment of the family surname around 1300. Most of these studies concern only lay men: women and clergy are generally few in number in the samples, and the methods of naming them were always archaic when compared to those affecting lay men.

In the Lombard charters of the eighth and ninth centuries, all the names were simple, often with a secondary element. The only evolution consists in the increasing use of the form *X filius Y* and in the correlative diminution of a professional or secondary legal qualification. Social differentiation was reflected in names given: the majority of the slaves and other

---

[6]Errico Cuozzo, "La militia Neapolitanorum: un modello per i milites normanni di Aversa," in MEFRM 107/1 (1995), pp. 31–38.

[7]Jean-Marie Martin, *Italies normandes. XIe–XIIe siècles* (Paris, 1994), pp. 278–79.

[8]Mario del Treppo and Alfonso Leone, *Amalfi medioevale* (Naples, 1977), pp. 89–119.

dependent peasants bore Roman (not Lombard) names. Clergymen had Christian names more often than lay people, probably because some of them were destined from birth to enter the clergy.

The rhythm of the imposition of the double name is very different in the Roman and Lombard regions. In Naples (which was never conquered by the Lombards), family surnames appeared as early as the beginning of the tenth century. They were still rare, but often hereditary (with the form *XZ filius YZ).* During the first half of the eleventh century, the double form became the more common, but the percentage remained stable during the following century. At that time there appeared the family surnames of many noble Neapolitan families (Capece, Caracciolo, Brancaccio). At the same time, the stock of personal names was very small and practically all of them were Christian (more than a quarter of the women were called *Mary*).

The very early use of a surname (already hereditary in some cases), as well as the unmistakably Christian character of the personal names, are both typical features of Latin-speaking Byzantine Italy: the case of Venice seems to be similar. In Naples, such a rapid (but not complete) evolution may be linked with the coherence of the family's patrimony, which is also expressed through the words *de illis Talibus* to indicate the properties of a family.

In the non-Byzantine regions, the situation was very different, although it was not exactly the same everywhere. The main point is that double naming came to predominate very much later, not only later than in Naples, but also than in France and even in northern Italy. The second feature (common with northern Italy) is the presence of numerous intermediate forms, such as *X filius YZ*, in which the surname is not given directly to the person in question, but to his father. In the same charter, the same person may be called *X filius Y* and *XY* (with the genitive for the second element) or *X de Y*.

In Troia (northern Apulia), double naming gained ascendancy about 1125, but for one century afterwards, the dominance of this double form was very marginal. In Bari (central Apulia), the predominance of the double form did not come before 1220, and indeed, the two Apulian cases are not very different from each other. The period 1120–1220 was in both cases a time of uncertainty. In Calabria and in Sicily, despite the scarcity of available documents, the pattern seems to have been similar; the triumph of the double form occurred about 1230 in Latin northern Calabria, in the first ten years of the thirteenth century in Messina and Catania (eastern Sicily) and between 1190 and 1220 in Palermo and Agrigento (western Sicily).

From the beginning of the thirteenth century the progression of the double form continued normally. In Palermo it accounted for 78 percent of the names of lay men from 1286 to 1287. In Bari, it accounted for 53 to 70 percent in the last third of the thirteenth century, and 65 to 80 percent in the first half of the fourteenth, depending on whether or not the form *X filius YZ*, which remained very important there, is taken into account.

It is difficult to determine why the surname and the double form came to predominate so much later in these regions. To be sure, the elements of the family's patrimony were not as precisely defined in the Lombard zones as they were in Naples or Amalfi, but indeed the devolution of the patrimony, if not exactly similar, was not profoundly different in the two cases. It must be added that, with the exception of Naples, Capua, and Palermo, the southern cities were generally rather small. Each inhabitant probably knew many of his fellow citizens.

Another factor is, as we shall see, that the stock of personal names was much richer in the Lombard areas than it was in Naples. It seems also that the notaries, who wrote the legal documents, had a conservative attitude, presumably believing that the only legal definition of a person consisted in his personal name, the name of his father, and the name of the place where he lived. Such a definition seems to have satisfied needs for a long time. The hesitation, for example, in the same document in Troia between *Iohannes de Sabbo* (double form) and *Iohannes filius Sabbi* (simple form) is a sign that the former was not automatically necessary. With regard to Sicily the explanations are still more difficult: the non-Muslim population of the island was mainly composed of recent immigrants from southern, but also northern, Italy.

In addition to this, one must point out that the great majority of surnames were patronymic names. Some of them were nicknames (also often
used as personal names) and surnames of toponymic origin were not infrequent. On the other hand, names from the professions were infrequent.
In Bari, the rare names of this type concerned offices or public charges, not
real professions, as for example *de Ammirato*, the surname of members of
the family of Maio of Bari, the great emir of William I. The mention of
the profession as a complement to the personal name, common among the
handicraftsmen, seems to indicate the actual profession of the person, thus
eliminating the need for a real surname. Such a pattern was still in effect
in Bari in the fourteenth century.

The feudal aristocracy, introduced by the Normans but including
Norman and Lombard families, had a distinctive attitude toward the surname, which was frequent and from early times represented a family
surname. It could be either the personal name of an ancestor, or the
toponymic name of the main fief. Sometimes it even included the place of
origin of the family in Normandy. The counts *de Molisio*, who gave their
name to the present administrative region of Molise, were the descendants
of the family of the Lords of Moulins-la-Marche in Normandy. And
sometimes in the eleventh and twelfth centuries the different branches of
a large feudal family changed their surname, taking as a new one the name
of the particular ancestor of the branch or that of a new fief. Such a
pattern was common outside southern Italy.

The final objective of our research was to measure the chronological
stages in the establishment of the surname as a real family surname at the
end of the thirteenth and at the beginning of the fourteenth centuries. In
Sicily (Messina and Palermo) the members of the feudal aristocracy and
of the richest non-feudal families frequently used a family surname (the
former preferring also certain personal names, such as the Maletta family,
linked by marriage with the Staufer). In Bari most of the family surnames
appeared during the thirteenth and fourteenth centuries; the hereditary
surname became common not only in the feudal dynasties, but also in the
families of notables, which gave the city its judges and the main churches

(the cathedral and St. Nicholas) some of their canons. Still it may be esti-
mated that less than a third of the population used a fixed family surname.

One recent study[9] gave original results from the analysis of lists of
peasants of the Abbey of Cava, near Salerno. Practically all of them were
designated by a hereditary family surname and, in one case at least, it can
be proved that such a surname was assigned by the monastic administration.

It seems indeed that the factors that explain the establishment of a
family surname are not simple. Certainly the self-consciousness of the family is one of them, and the settling on such names first in feudal dynasties,
then in families of urban notables, is not a matter of chance. However, one
must stress the importance of external factors, specifically of political and
administrative origin. The case of the peasants of Cava is very clear from
this point of view. One may also suppose that the apparently higher rate
of family surnames in the Sicilian cities compared to that in Bari is to be
related to the composite population of Sicily, and particularly of its main
centers, whereas Bari has preserved its old families of notables of Lombard
origin. In addition to this, the Angevin Régime gave the cities a higher
degree of self-government, thus limiting administrative interference.

The last point concerns the nature of the personal names. Like the
inhabitants of Naples, who used a small number of purely Christian names,
the Greek population of Salento (southern Apulia) used a stock of Christian names that were mainly, but not exclusively, of Greek origin. On the
other hand, in the Lombard regions, Germanic names were predominant:
two-thirds in the eighth and ninth centuries, followed by Romanic (20
percent) and Christian and biblical ones (14 percent). The subsequent
evolution was not linear. Apparently the main tendency was towards the
christianization of names, but the arrival of the Normans, like the immi-
gration of northern Lombards in Sicily, brought new Germanic names
(*Roger, Richard, William*) which, at least from the twelfth century, were
not reserved for the Norman aristocracy. Besides, as in other Italian regions,

---

[9]Villani, "L'antroponimia rurale."

Romanic nicknames with a positive or negative value (*Armisdoctus, Maluscor*) appeared as personal names in the twelfth and thirteenth centuries.

Christianization itself was neither exclusive nor simple. While the main names of the New Testament took first place (*John* was most used everywhere), Greek Christian names were also not rare in Lombard Apulia under Byzantine rule and even later. The names of purely local saints were rarely given (*Ianuarius*, or *Gennaro*, who was already venerated in Naples, did not give his name to the citizens). On the contrary, people used the names of important saints whose relics had been transferred, or were supposed to have been transferred, into the region, such as *Nicholas* (Bari), *Matthew* (Salerno), and *Bartholomew* (Benevento).

There is no obvious relationship between a possible restriction of the number of different personal names and the increased use of surnames. In Troia, the number of personal names increased. The three most popular, which in the eleventh century were used by 43 percent of the population, were borne by only 22 percent in the thirteenth century. Generally, however, the evolution went the other way, but even in this case, there is no precise coincidence between the restriction of the number of names and the increase of the surnames. Such a relation probably exists, but only indirectly.

The same conclusion concerns the relationship between anthroponomy and family structure. The hypothesis of a direct link between one and the other is reinforced by the very early rise of the surname, and even of the family surname in Naples, a city in which the use of Roman law gave more solidity to the family patrimony, and the priority of the upper social classes. But even in these cases, anthroponomy seems to reflect family consciousness more than actual family structure—the consciousness being linked with the wealth of the family. But outside the family, one must not forget the importance of external factors, political and administrative, and above all the purely cultural factors. The Apulians with barbarian names were not less Christian than the Neapolitans. The most direct relationship is probably to be found between names used and laws of persons.

PART IV

PERSONAL NAMES AND CULTURAL CONTACTS

Personal Names, Immigration, and Cultural Change: *Francos* and Muslims in the Medieval Crown of Aragon

Carlos Laliena

An anonymous writer at the beginning of the twelfth century, referring to the foundation of the small village of Sahagún, near León, said that it had been populated by "people of diverse and strange provinces and kingdoms, that is, Gascons, Bretons, Germans, English, Burgundians, Normans, Tuscans, Provençals, Lombards, and many other merchants from different countries and strange tongues."[1] He is writing about the European immigrants who settled in the cities created along the pilgrim's road to Santiago or in the cities taken over from Islam at the end of the eleventh century. In Castile and León as well as in Aragon, sources refer to these people with an ethnic denomination, *francos*, which reflects, as was demonstrated fifty years ago by Charles Higounet, that they principally came from the south of France.[2] The importance of these "foreign

---

[1] *Crónicas anónimas de Sahagún*, ed. Antonio Ubieto Arteta (Zaragoza, 1987), pp. 19–21: "Como el sobredicho rei ordenase e estableçiese que aí se fiçiese villa, ayuntáronse de todas partes del uniberso burgueses de muchos e diversos ofiçios, conbiene a saver, herreros, carpinteros, xastres, pelliteros, çapateros, escutarios e omes enseñados en muchas e dibersas artes e ofiçios. E otrosi personas de diversas e estrañas provinçias e reinos, conbiene a saver, gascones, bretones, alemanes, yngleses, normandos, tolosanos, provinçiales, lonbardos e muchos otros negoçiadores de diversas naçiones e estrannas lenguas."

[2] Jean Gautier-Dalché, *Historia urbana de León y Castilla en la Edad Media (siglos IX–XIII)* (Madrid, 1979); Juan Carrasco Pérez, "El Camino navarro a Compostela: los espacios urbanos (siglos XII–XV)," in *Las peregrinaciones a Santiago de Compostela y San Salvador de Oviedo en la Edad Media*, ed. Juan Ignacio Ruiz de la Peña (Oviedo, 1993), pp. 103–07; Pascual Martínez Sopena, "Logroño y las villas riojanas entre los siglos XII y XIV," in

peoples" or foreigners was decisive in the configuration of the urban societies of the northern part of the Iberian Peninsula, as is shown by how quickly regal authority conferred privileged status on them. The case of Toledo is well known, but, to cite another example, we can mention what happened in Huesca, a town conquered in 1096, where the influence of the *francos* started so early and with such intensity that in 1100 the king of Aragon, Pedro I, issued a special concession (*cartam ingenuitatis*) that embraced the immigrants of the Pyrenees as well as any foreigner with French origins.[3] In probably less than 30 years, the *francos* had come to constitute at least a third of the inhabitants of the town.

Let us look at another example. In 1137, everyone in Jaca, a small town in the north of Aragon found on the route to Santiago, had to swear allegiance to its new sovereign, Ramón Berenguer IV. A total of 189 did, of which only about ten had names that indicated an Aragonese origin, while the rest had names that suggest that they were *francos*.[4]

Historia de la ciudad de Logroño, ed. José Angel Sesma Muñoz, vol. 2 (Logroño, 1995), pp. 279–322, and "Repoblaciones interiores, villas nuevas de los siglos XII y XIII," in *Despoblación y colonización del Valle del Duero, siglos XII–XX* (Madrid, 1995), pp. 163–87. In relation to the *francos*, José María Lacarra, "A propos de la colonisation 'franca' en Navarra et en Aragón," *Annales du Midi* 65 (1953), 331–42; Charles Higounet, "Mouvements de population dans le Midi de la France du XIe au XVe siècle, d'après les noms de personne et de lieu," in *Paysages et villages neufs du Moyen Age*, ed. Higounet (Bordeaux, 1975), pp. 417–37; Juan Ignacio Ruiz de la Peña Solar, "Las colonizaciones francas en las rutas castellano-leonesas del Camino de Santiago," in *Las peregrinaciones*, ed. Ruiz de la Peña, pp. 283–312.

[3]Jean Pierre Molenat, "Quartiers et communautés à Tolède (XIIe–XVe siècles)," *En la España Medieval* 12 (1989), 163–89; Antonio García Gallo, "Los Fueros de Toledo," *Anuario de Historia del Derecho Español* 45 (1975), 341–488, esp. 467–68. About Huesca, see *Documentos Municipales de Huesca, 1100–1350*, ed. Carlos Laliena Corbera (Huesca, 1988).

[4]Antonio Ubieto Arteta, "Sobre demografia aragonesa del siglo XII," in *Quince temas medievales publicados por el profesor Don Antonio Ubieto*, ed. Ubieto Arteta (Zaragoza, 1991), pp. 219–39; Lynn H. Nelson, "Personal Name Analysis of Limited Bases of Data: Examples of Applications to Medieval Aragonese History," *Historical Methods. A Journal*

This makes clear to us the enormous utility of personal naming for detecting the presence of those immigrants in Hispanic towns and cities. Continuing with the example of Jaca, it is easy to deduce that people called *Bartolomeu de Cahors, Ramon de Condom* or *Gocelm de Montpellier* came from Toulouse, Gascony, or Languedoc. We can also be reasonably sure that people named *Roger* or *Osmond* were from Normandy, while others, such as *Pere Archimbald*, were perhaps Italians. But certainly also *Ubert, Ebrard, Aimerig, Tebald,* or *Peitavis* among many that could be cited, are undoubtedly socially different from an ethnic point of view from the Aragonese peasants, whose names were generally chosen from among the archaic Basque names of *Sancho, Garcia, Iñigo,* or *Jimeno,* and they respected faithfully the model of the *nomina paterna* (Christian name plus the name of the father in the genitive case to indicate family ties). By contrast, the *francos* often used only one name or the Christian name accompanied by a second name in the nominative case (which could also be considered a *nomen paternum* but this is not certain) but the most distinctive was the use of names accompanied by indications of geographic origins, or names with indications of artisanal occupation.[5]

This personal naming model peculiar to the *francos* was the result of their emigration and the cultural rupture they experienced: enrolled in a new society, at times very far from their native countries, they were recognized simply by their Christian names, which in themselves were most exotic. When it appears that a more precise means of identification was necessary, the second element of designation was the place the person

---

of Quantitative and Interdisciplinary History 24 (1991), 4–15. On the context of this oath, see Thomas N. Bisson, "The Problem of Feudal Monarchy: Aragon, Catalonia, France," *Speculum* 53 (1978), 460–78.

[5]Carlos Laliena Corbera, "Los sistemas antroponomicos en Aragón durante los siglos XI y XII," in *Antroponimia y sociedad. Sistemas de identificacion hispano-cristianos en los siglos IX a XIII,* ed. Pascual Martínez Sopena (Santiago de Compostela-Valladolid, 1995), pp. 297–326; and Juan Ignacio Ruiz de la Peña Solar, "La antroponimia como indicador de fenómenos de movilidad geografica: el ejemplo de las colonizaciones francas en el Oviedo medieval (1100–1230)," ibid., pp. 133–54.

came from. For example *Sanc, cabater de Tolosa*, was "Sanz, shoemaker of Toulouse." A name might also refer to their work: *Rogger, cabater*, "Roger, shoemaker," or *Aimerig, mercer*, "Aimeric, merchant." This latter trend is very significant, since the *francos* settled almost exclusively in urban nuclei and took on basically artisan or merchant activities.

In Jaca, a fourth of these inhabitants of French origin had a second name alluding to a craft and among these the shoemakers stood out. In fact, for a peasant embarking on a long journey seduced by the "castles in Spain," the easiest trade, requiring the least specialization and the cheapest tools, was the making of shoes. But there were also merchants and money changers dazzled by the business done in large towns like León, Burgos, Oviedo, Toledo, or Zaragoza, taken from the Muslims, or along the routes traveled by pilgrims to Santiago de Compostela.

The cultural integration of these immigrant *francos* was without doubt slow. A prosopography of the *francos* of Huesca, one of the towns with the fullest documentation for the twelfth century, demonstrates how the *francos* preferred to establish ties within this social group. One that merits special consideration within the urban society of this town is Don Robin, tanner, who had a son-in-law called Don Hugas, *zabater*, "Don Hugo, shoemaker," also a *franco*. The choice of names for descendants reveals the same concern with maintaining a certain degree of social identity: the son of Paian Rossel is named *Andreu*, the son of Don Ofre is named *Don Espanol*, *Jordan* is the son of Pere Pictavin, and examples of this preference for unusual names could be expanded upon. It is also interesting to note that when *francos* were involved in legal action, the guarantors and the witnesses were almost always *francos*, too.[6]

In some towns, this solidarity was also strengthened by the grouping of the *francos'* residences in the same suburb or street, a more frequent practice in León and Galicia. Economic activities, legal statutes, residence, the formation of family ties, and the network of informal relationships

---

[6]The examples come from Antonio Durán Gudiol, *Colección diplomática de la Catedral de Huesca*, vol. 1 (Zaragoza, 1965).

were all intended to preserve the collective identity of the *francos*. But none of it could have survived throughout the twelfth century without the existence of a special personal naming system. It is not by chance that, while there was a huge growth in names like *Pedro, Juan,* and *Domingo,* the *francos* preserved names such as *Galacian, Aquelmes, Aimeric, Paian, Raol,* as well as *Guillem, Ramo,* or *Martin,* which were a little more common. As can be seen, this was an onomastic model full of rather varied names extracted from the name stock of the European regions to the north of the Pyrenees, which the *francos* strove to preserve for three to four generations before merging definitively into a much more homogenous society in the thirteenth century.

The *francos* are not the only social group embedded within the dynamic population of the countries of the Crown of Aragon. From the twelfth century onward, the conquering of the Muslim lands of al-Andalus (the Islamic part of the Iberian Peninsula) meant the incorporation of large contingents of Muslim peasants into the feudal societies.[7] Historians use the expression *mudéjares,* which comes from an Arabic word meaning "tributaries," to refer to them. Their distribution is very uneven, and in the same way that Islamic elements are almost non-existent in Castile and León, they are abundant in some regions of the Ebro Valley, in Aragon as well as in Catalonia and Valencia. In the latter region towards the end of the fifteenth century, one in every four inhabitants was Muslim.[8] Naturally there are fundamental differences with regard to the *francos*: the Muslims lived mainly in the rural areas and were peasants, while the

---

[7]John Boswell, *The Royal Treasure: Muslim Communities under the Crown of Aragon in the Fourteenth Century* (New Haven, 1977).

[8]Miguel Angel Ladero Quesada, "Los mudéjares de Castilla en la Baja Edad Media," in *Los mudéjares de Castilla y otros estudios de historia medieval andaluza,* ed. Ladero Quesada (Granada, 1989), pp. 11–132; Mark Meyerson, *The Muslims of Valencia in the Age of Fernando and Isabel: Between Coexistence and Crusade* (Berkeley, 1991); José María Lacarra, "Introducción al estudio de los mudéjares aragoneses," in *Aragón en la Edad Media. Estudios de economía y sociedad,* vol. 2 (Zaragoza, 1979), pp. 7–23.

francos lived in the towns and cities and were merchants and craftsmen, and, above all, the Muslims constituted an unassimilable minority because of the characteristics of their religion, their culture, and their way of life. We should stress this latter aspect, which is decisive: protected by the kings and nobles, the Muslims were subject to severe ethnic discrimination, against which they protected themselves above all by the solidarity, the coherency, and the impenetrability of their rural communities. Having taken refuge in these, they endured a relationship with the Christians that was plagued by humiliations, but one that nonetheless never developed into one of true ideological pressure or of religious persecution until the sixteenth century. The Muslims thus became a peculiar society formed by a large minority both discriminated against and a prisoner of its own culture.

Among the distinctive features of this culture was its personal naming system. As we know, the Arabic personal naming systems are very complex and based on two models: the recognition of genealogy and of the onomastic elements of relationship (geographical origins, indication of occupation, tribal bonds, and personal or affective relationships).[9] The result is that the designation of an individual transmits a large amount of information in the form of a long chain of names of ancestors united by a personal name (what is called *nasab* or affiliation). This chain is usually preceded by a name that indicates a paternal or filial relationship, the *kunya*, and generally ends with a name that suggests a geographical or tribal bond and that is called *nisba*. Theoretically, this personal naming model emphasizes the family relationship more than the individuality of each person and is characterized by locating people in the context of their clan and lineage.[10] It is very important to point out that for the Muslims, names are significant. The Prophet himself insisted on this and in the Koran said, "God has beautiful names, praise him by using them."

---

[9]Jacqueline Sublet, *Le voile du nom. Essai sur le nom propre arabe* (Vendôme, 1991).

[10]Jacqueline Sublet, "Nom et identité dans le monde musulman," in *L'anthroponymie. Document de l'histoire sociale des mondes méditerranéens médiévaux*, ed. Monique Bourin, Jean-Marie Martin, and François Menant (Rome, 1996), pp. 97–108.

Therefore it is necessary to be careful in interpreting this complicated system of designating people.

The first question we should ask is whether the Muslims maintained this sophisticated model after being forcefully integrated into a massively Christian society. The answer, from my perspective, is affirmative.[11] Although they are not numerous, we still have some documents written in Arabic from the mid-twelfth century to the end of the fifteenth century, and in them there is a sufficient number of names to be able to prove that the traditional features of the Arabic naming system remained in use within the *mudéjar* society until the end of the Middle Ages.[12] We can even state that in Valencia this phenomenon of preservation was greater than in other regions such as in the Valley of the Ebro.[13] However, it is probable that, as time passed, the traditional model was used basically as a form of conveying prestige by the people of a higher rank or social class, while the normal system of designation was notably simplified. Therefore it is perfectly possible to find people named, to quote a concrete example from Aragon in the last years of the fifteenth century: *Abu l-Hasan* (the *kunya*) *'Ali* (the *ism* or proper name) *ibn Sa'id ibn Ballas* (the *nasab* or

---

[11]Carlos Laliena Corbera, "La antroponimia de los mudejares: resistencia y aculturacion de una minoría étnico-religiosa," in *L'anthroponymie. Document de l'histoire sociale*, ed. Bourin et al., pp. 142–66. Pierre Guichard, "L'anthroponymie des zones en contact entre monde chrétien et monde musulman: de Palerme à Tolède," ibid., pp. 109–22.

[12]Jacinto Bosch Vilá, "Los documentos árabes del archivo catedral de Huesca," *Revista del Instituto de Estudios Islámicos en Madrid* 5 (1957), 1–48; Mercedes García Arenal, "Documentos Árabes de Tudela y Tarazona," *Al-Qantara* 3 (1982), 26–72; María Jesús Viguera Molins, "Dos nuevos documentos árabes de Aragón (Jarque y Morés, 1492)," *Aragón en la Edad Media* 4 (1981), 231–65; Ana Labarta, "Reconocimiento de tutela a un mudéjar de Daroca (documento árabe de 1477)," *Aragón en la Edad Media* 5 (1983), 207–17, and "La aljama de los musulmanes de Calatorao nombra procurador (documento árabe de 1451)," *Al-Qantara* 9 (1988), 511–17; Wilhelm Hoenerbach, *Spanische-Islamische Urkunden aus der Zeit der Nasriden und Moriscos* (Bonn, 1965).

[13]María del Carmen Barceló Torres, *Minorías islámicas en el País Valenciano. Historia y dialecto* (Valencia, 1984); Ana Labarta, *La onomástica de los moriscos valencianos* (Madrid, 1987).

genealogy). That is, Abul-Hasan ʿAli ibn Saʿid ibn Ballas, with a geo-graphical or tribal *nisba* ("al-Saraqusti," for example, "from Zaragoza," or "al-Lahmi," "from the Lahmies," the name of an Arab tribe). But the most normal procedure was to reduce the name down to two elements, nor-mally the proper name or *ism* followed by the *nasab* as in "Mohammed ibn Lubb," i.e., "Mohammed, son of Lubb," or by the *nisba*, as in "Mo-hammed al-Qurtubi," i.e., "Mohammed from Cordoba."

This simplification, which is in any case not unusual since in the classical age of Islam it must have been in daily use, was probably accen-tuated by Christian influence. Thus it is appropriate to remember that from the twelfth century onward, a naming system of two elements, a name and a surname, held sway in Christian societies. The second name tended to convert more or less into a fixed family name.[14] It is possible, though this problem will have to be investigated more thoroughly, that the reduction of the Arab names of the *mudéjares* was a consequence of a rough adaptation of their family organization to the dominant form of the Christian world based on a small family nucleus and marital monog-amy. This adaptation could be very similar to what the *mudejars* were obliged to do in other matters such as the political organization of their communities or *aljamas*.

The Muslim communities formed, as I have said, compact social units that were very difficult for the Christians to penetrate. But the *mudejars* sometimes lived together with the Christians, went to the same markets, worked for them, or paid taxes to the king's tax collectors to their feudal lords. These contacts required that the Christians know the names of the Muslims with whom they dealt. And this raises an interesting problem of cultural relationships between two ethnic groups separated by enormous differences. To offer an example of this sort of problem toward the end of the thirteenth century, the Christian authorities pro-hibited the use of *algarabia* (the Arabic spoken by the *mudéjares*) in business transactions in the urban markets in order to avoid fraud and

---

[14]*Antroponimia y sociedad*, ed. Martínez Sopena.

misinterpretations.[15] If these people spoke different languages, we can ask how the Christians understood Muslim names.

In Tudela, a town near Zaragoza on the banks of the River Ebro, there was an important Muslim quarter in the twelfth century for which some documents written in Arabic survive for the years 1167–77, and which are exceptional because of Latin interlinear translation in the same texts.[16] In this way we can compare the names taken by the Muslims in question to those written and given to them by the Christians. For example, a person who figures in these documents is called *Ahmed ibn Moham-med al-Balmi*, a perfectly traditional name, with his genealogical *nasab* and his *nisba* or his family clan name ("al-Balmi"). But the Christian translator limited himself to calling this man *Hamet Alpelme* ("Ahmad al-Balmi"), thereby omitting the genealogical element. Another longer example: *Mo-hammed ibn Ahmad ibn Mohammed al Bahini* became *Alpelini alcadi* ("al-Bahini al-qadi"). In this case the translator selected took only the *nisba* and added to this the function this man fulfilled in the Muslim community, *alcadi*, i.e., "judge." Thus we can see that the Christians eliminated those name elements that got in their way and left just two components for the purpose of identification. Put another way, they applied their own personal naming model.

In the fourteenth and fifteenth centuries, this phenomenon acquired a most curious trait. For that period large lists are available of Muslim names written by Christian notaries for different circumstances, but above all for the assembly meetings of the *aljamas* or the Islamic communities.[17] The documents are in Old Spanish and the names are written as understood by the Christians. In these we can see notable differences with respect to the classic Arab model.

---

[15] *Documentos municipales*, ed. Laliena Corbera.

[16] García Arenal, "Documentos Árabes."

[17] Francisco Macho Ortega, "Condición social de los mudéjares aragoneses (siglo XV)," in *Memorias de la Facultad de Filosofía y Letras de la Universidad de Zaragoza*, vol. 1 (Zaragoza, 1923), pp. 137–368.

For the Christians, the Muslims always have two names: a personal name, almost always *Mahoma, Juce,* or *Ibrahim,* and a second name taken from a place name, a trade name, or a nickname. For example, *Mahoma de Murviedro, Mahoma the Castillian* (place names), *Mahoma the Bald,* or *the Blonde,* or *the Lefty,* or *the Chacho* (*al-Hayy,* i.e., he who had traveled to Mecca on pilgrimage), *Mahoma Zauzala* (*sahib al-sahla,* i.e., the prayer caller), *Mahoma Alfaqui* (the expert in law), etc. Sometimes these names coincided with or translated into the actual names of the Muslims. For example, one *Abd Allah al Sultan* became "Audalla el Rey," or Abdallah the King, and one *Abd al-Rahman al-Ahmar* became "Durramen el Royo," or *Abd al-Rahman the Blond* or *the Red-Haired.* But frequently the Christians did not take into account the authentic names and assigned Muslims names related to their place of origin or to their personal or family characteristics. However, these surnames were limited in variety and some frequently-used nicknames were slightly disdainful. But the truth is that the *mudéjares* accepted the use of these names in their dealings with the Christians and took them as their own. From my point of view, this amounted to a form of cultural or social resistance.

By accepting these designations, the Muslims protected their true names; the aliases given to them by the Christians were useful because they allowed them to protect this bastion of privacy which was very important to them, as shown by Jacqueline Sublet.[18] Besides, in using these often-repeated names, individuality was hidden and identification by Christians was made difficult. In this way, informal contacts outside official channels were impeded. These names veiled the names of the Muslims and helped them to maintain their social identity.

---

[18]Sublet, *Le voile du nom.*

FAMILIES OF OUTREMER: A SOURCE OF TRADITIONAL NAMING CUSTOMS

Marie-Adelaïde Nielen

A genealogical document, the *Lignages d'Outremer*,[1] inserted into a group of juridical texts called *The Assises of Jerusalem,* is the source of this study.[2] The first version was written circa 1270,[3] then expanded around 1306–07,[4] and was modified a few more times later on. This document presents a great resource for prosopographical research because it offers both a precise chronological frame (the beginning of the twelfth century to the beginning of the fourteenth century) and a defined geographical and political one as well: the Latin States of the East.

In this article I am using the second version of this text (the Latin manuscript 4789 of the Biblioteca Vaticana), which deals with about forty

---

[1]Only Portugal seems to have genealogical texts as important as the *Lignages d'Outremer*, with the *Livro velho de linhagens*, written about 1270, the *Livro de linhagens do Deão* and the *Livro de linhagens do Conde D. Pedro*. Joseph M. Piel and José Mattoso, eds., *Portugaliae monumenta historica*, vol. 1, *Livros velhos de linhagens*, ed. Piel and Mattoso (Lisbon, 1980), and vol. 2, *Livro de linhagens do Conde D. Pedro*, ed. Mattoso (Lisbon, 1980). On these, see Mattoso, "La littérature généalogique et la culture de la noblesse au Portugal (XIIIe–XIVe siècles)," *Bulletin des Études Portugaises et Brésiliennes* 44–45 (1985), 73–92, and Robert Durand, "Trois siècles de dénomination aristocratique portugaise d'après la littérature généalogique," in *Genèse médiévale de l'anthroponymie moderne. III. Enquêtes généalogiques et données prosopographiques*, ed. Monique Bourin and Pascal Chareille (1995), pp. 43–54.

[2]See my paper, "Un livre méconnu des Assises de Jérusalem: les Lignages d'Outremer," *Bibliothèque de l'Ecole des Chartes* 153 (January–June 1995), 103–30.

[3]Venice, Biblioteca Marciana, MS Francesi 20[(265)].

[4]Vatican City, Biblioteca Apostolica Vaticana, MS Vat. lat. 4789.

families of the Latin East and their marriages. It includes the kings of Jerusalem, the smallest lineages, and those of the great barons as well. It cites nearly 1,300 persons: 805 men and 479 women. One hundred and eighty-three first names are enough to name these 1,300 persons, including 114 masculine names and sixty-nine feminine ones.

Of course this source is far from infallible. Names can be inverted and generations confused, and that is not to mention the great uncertainty surrounding the first generations, which, until the middle of the twelfth century, or even until the last quarter of it, are at best unreliable.

Fortunately, in numerous cases the acts found in the cartularies from the Holy Land help to confirm these genealogies.[5] Apart from the stated reservations, we have the good fortune to have forty genealogies, as complete and coherent as possible. This allows us to study the naming policy of the families of the Holy Land. Was their policy very different from the one followed in the West? Did Latin settlers arrive in the Holy Land with their own stock of names? Was this stock modified on the spot, or did it remain stable? What was the role of parenthood in naming? Did feminine names follow the same rules as masculine ones? What role did maternal lineage take in naming practices? In this study I hope to give some answers to these questions.

Fashionable Masculine Names

Among the 114 masculine first names given in the *Lignages d'Outremer,* some occur very often, being attributed to at least twenty persons. This enables us to establish a list of twelve names which are borne by 480 men, or more than 50 percent of the total. These names are: *John, Hugh, William, Baldwin, Philip, Guy, Balian, Raymond, Amalric* or *Aimery, Walter, Peter,* and *Thomas.* We see that the choice is usually a classic one and also that the names fashionable in the East are also fashionable in the West.

---

[5]Reinhold Röhricht, *Regesta regni Hierosolymitani, 1097–1291* (Innsbruck, 1893), and *Additamentum* (Innsbruck, 1904).

This tends to show that Latin lords established in the Holy Land brought western customs and fashions along with them and that they did not change. Let us consider for example a name given forty times: *Baldwin*. This is a common name in the West, although it is rare outside Flanders and Artois. Its vogue in the Holy Land is easy to explain as it was the name of several kings of Jerusalem.

Among this list of standard names *Balian* represents an exception. It is completely unknown in French anthroponomy, even though the lords of Ibelin who brought it to the Holy Land claimed to come from the Viscounts of Chartres.[6] Its origin is unknown but is probably Italian. It can be found in Liguria and in Sardinia. It was introduced to the Holy Land in the first half of the twelfth century by Balian *à la barbe* ("the bearded"), also known as Balian the Frenchman, first Lord of Ibelin. Initially it was given only to members of this family but it later spread to other lineages through matrimonial ties and probably also because of the extraordinary social rise of this family. The case of the name *Balian* is spectacular. On the other hand, some names borne by illustrious people did not spread at all: *Godfrey*, for example, the name of the leader of the first crusade, or *Bohemond*, which was extremely rare outside of the princely family of Antioch. The reason for this might have been that these names were quickly disliked or thought to be out of date.

In any case it can be noted that heroes, whether mythical or real, have almost no role in the spread of names. At the beginning of the fourteenth century, when our text comes to an end, there are very few names inspired by romantic characters. There is only one *Lancelot* and two *Roland*s.

In the cases of other names it is difficult to tell exactly why they were given so often. Let us take the case of the name *John*. It is as common in the West as in the East, proving that exchanges between these two parts of the world were numerous and even that naming customs moved around.

---

[6]On this alleged origin and on the name of Balian, see Jean Richard, "Guy d'Ibelin, O.P., évêque de Limassol, et l'inventaire de ses biens," *Bulletin de correspondance hellénique* 74 (1950), 98–133; Wipertus-Hugo Rüdt de Collenberg, "Les Ibelins aux XIIIe–XIVe siècles," *Epeteris* 9 (1977–79), 117–265 and "Les premiers Ibelins," *Le Moyen Age* (1965), 433–74.

Furthermore, *John* is the name of the father of Maria Comnena, first wife of King Amalric of Jerusalem and then of Balian of Ibelin. Throughout the thirteenth and fourteenth centuries *John* continued to be a name given at almost every generation in the Ibelin family. For this name contemporary fashion as well as reference to an ancestor played a role in its diffusion.

Originality or Family Names?

As I said, twelve different names are sufficient for 480 men. But what about the 325 others sharing 102 names? Forty-two names are given only once. Others, although occurring fewer than ten times, remain quite traditional: *Anciau, Bertrand, Eustace, Nicolas, Gilles*, or *Simon*. That others are even less frequent is not surprising: *Bernard, Gerard, Thibaut*, or *Robert* are in fact rare. Why do these names so commonly given in some parts of France remain exceptional in the Holy Land?

Other names, perhaps even rarer, are mandatory as the leading names of lineages. Thus, along with Balian of Ibelin and Bohemond of Antioch, we find Humphrey of Toron, Joscelin of Edessa, Daniel of Adelon, Lawrence of Morf, Angelier of Gibelet, Rostaing of Botrun, Gormond of Bethsan,[7] Melior of Maraclée,[8] and Rohard of Cayphas. These are certainly names brought to the Holy Land by these crusaders' families that were never completely dropped, and continued to be passed on from father to son or grandfather to grandson for three or four generations. The Holy Land appears truly to have been a place for the preservation of personal names.

Regional customs have an important influence: each group came with its stock of names from its region of origin, and kept them without

---

[7] On the family of Bethsan, see John L. La Monte and Norton Downs, "The Lords of Bethsan in the Kingdoms of Jerusalem and Cyprus," *Medievalia et Humanistica* 6 (1950), 57–75.

[8] On the family of Maraclée, see Wipertus-Hugo Rüdt de Collenberg, "Les Raynouard, seigneurs de Néfin et de Maraclé en terre sainte et leur parenté en Languedoc," *Cahiers de civilisation médiévale* 7/3 (1964), 289–311.

many changes. *Rostaing*, quite frequent in southern France, is given only in the Languedoc family of Boutron. *Eustace*, common in northern France, is rare outside of the Flemish family that held the lordships of Sidon and Caesarea.[9]

Did the intermingling of populations from very different origins bring changes in the choice of names? In fact, the answer is that this was very seldom the case. The names of traditional eastern saints are almost never given in these families. Even after some intermarriage Greek names are not adopted, nor do weddings between Franks and Italians alter the stock of names.

On the other hand, Armenian names sometimes spread into Frankish families following marriages: *Thoros* or *Roupen* are often given to Latin men. Conversely, Frankish names also spread into Armenian lineages.[10]

The Transmission of First Names within the Family

The text says *"Et le tiers avoit nom Gui come son père"* ("and the third child bore the name Gui like his father"),[11] which is an explicit reference to the choice of a name in memory of the father. This is not the most common way of naming, however, for usually it is the grandfather's name that prevails. In the Ibelin lineage there is a stock of customary names. At the time of the origin of the lineage (the beginning of the twelfth century), we find three names: *Balian*, *Baldwin*, and *Hugh*. All three of them are given repeatedly to everyone of the subsequent five generations. At the end of the twelfth century, three new names appear: *Jean*, *Philip*, and *Guy*, at the initiative of the maternal lineage. This sequence becomes stereotyped

---

[9]On the families of Sidon and Caesarea, see John L. La Monte, "The Lords of Caesarea in the Period of the Crusades," *Speculum* 22 (1947), 145–61, and "The Lords of Sidon," *Byzantion* 17 (1944–45), 183–211.

[10]On the Armenian lineages, see Wipertus-Hugo Rüdt de Collenberg, *The Rupenides, Hethumides and Lusignans. The Structure of the Armeno-Cilician Dynasties* (Paris, 1963).

[11]Venice, Biblioteca Marciana, MS Francesi 20[(265)], fol. 191.

and very few are the members of this lineage who deviate from these three choices. More often, it is the paternal grandfather's name that prevails for the eldest son. Then come the names of uncles or great-uncles. The father's name is very seldom chosen and then only for the third or the fourth son. In only four cases did sons receive their maternal grandfather's name (*Thomas, Thoros, Aimery,* and *Walter*).

In many other lineages, we find the same alternation between grandfather and grandson, giving a succession of names like *Adam / Gormond / Adam / Gormond* in the Bethsan family or *Hugh / Bertrand / Hugh / Bertrand* in that of the Gibelet. Others seem to have preferred a family name given from father to son like Joscelin at Edessa or Walter at Caesarea. For the choice of names as well as for the way in which they were handed down, customs seem to have been quite traditional, all of them probably having been imported from the West.

Feminine Names

The *Lignages d'Outremer* list 479 women who share sixty-nine names. The selection seems a bit larger than that available for men, given the fact that although there are about half as many women as men in the text, there are more than half as many different feminine first names. But the selection is a traditional one: eight names are given to more than twenty persons and five of these are given to 252 women, or more than half the total. These five names, *Isabella, Mary, Margaret, Alice,* and *Agnes,* are also very common in the West during the twelfth and thirteenth centuries. All of them have been given in the royal family of Jerusalem. On the other hand, *Melisende,* name of the first queen of Jerusalem, remains rare.

Just as was true for the men, so we have seen that very few names, ten at the most, suffice to name most of the women cited in the text. What about the fifty-nine other names?

A first group can be made out of names quite frequent in the West and which can also be found in the East. These names, even though less common than *Isabella* or *Mary,* do not seem strange nor original. We can cite *Sibyl, Beatrice, Philippa,* or *Douce.* Even less frequent but still known, *Constance, Simone,* and *Lucy,* are found periodically along with a few *Ancelles, Bienvenues,* or *Hodiernas.* From this not-exhaustive list it can be noted that Germanic names have little attraction: we find few *Mathildes, Berthes, Raymondes,* or *Richeuts.* The only popular Germanic name is *Alice,* which thrived, particularly in the thirteenth century.

Still, what seems to be striking about women's names is the relative freedom that existed in the parents' choice, a freedom that did not seem to exist for men. It is as if the choice for girls could be more easily freed from the rules imposed by the lineage. That is why we find *Chandeleur* (Candlemas), *Beduine* (who gets her name from that of her lineage), as well as *Bourgogne* or *Poitevine.* Some other rare names seem to be nicknames given according to the supposed character of the child. We find one *Suave* (Sweet), three *Tourterelles* (turtledove), three *Plaisances* (pleasant), and even two *Orgueilleuses* (proud).

Some names remain very rare and cannot be linked to any group. These include *Orable, Ofane,* or *Macee*; sometimes names also appear to be feminized versions of men's names, like *Thomasse* or *Luque.* Even though one cannot note any real originality in the choice of feminine names, it seems that usages for girls are less restrictive than they are for boys. Most of these women's names were imported from the West by the crusaders. Some of them, however, appear to be rare in the West and more widespread in the East. Names like *Eschiva, Helvis,* and *Stephanie,* for example, are very much in favor among the families of the Latin East that use them from the twelfth to the fourteenth century. These are imported names. As was true for men's names, there was very little borrowing on the spot.

Armenian first names, like those of two queens of Jerusalem, *Arda* and *Morfia,* did not spread widely. The same held true for Greek names. For women as well as for men, we do not find innovation. One exception must be noted though, and that is the name *Euphemia,* typically a Greek name, which became quite popular among the families of the Latin East. Unfortunately, it is impossible to find any reason to explain its relative success.

Women's Role in Family Naming

Even though difficult to measure, it is obvious that women sometimes had a role in naming. There is one very convincing example of the
influence of the maternal lineage in the selection of names. The only son
born to Reynald, Lord of Sidon (who came from one of the oldest and
most powerful families in the Holy Land) and his wife, Helvis of Ibelin,
daughter of Balian the First, was named Balian.[12] The maternal lineage
imposed its choice. Examples of the name type, whether involving the
eldest son or one of the younger ones, are numerous, and show that the
maternal lineage has a certain importance in the naming of boys. We must
remember that we are in a very closed society, chiefly oriented towards war
that is often deadly. Lordships were often transmitted by women.

But a clear preponderance of the paternal lineage can also be noted
in the selection of girls' names, for the eldest daughter often bears her
paternal grandmother's name. We can see that in the family of the Princes
of Antioch, the daughter who seems to be the eldest is invariably named
after her paternal grandmother, with only one exception, over eight generations. We can name further examples of this kind, even though this rule
does not strictly apply to every generation.

The maternal grandmother's name does not appear as often, though
it is also given. In the family of Tiberias, *Eschiva*, often transmitted by
women, is used frequently and was the name of a noble ancestor of
Tiberias in the middle of the twelfth century.[13] It seems that generally
speaking the eldest daughter bears the name of her maternal grandmother
or, more often, of her paternal grandmother. This rule applies to very common names like *Margaret* or *Isabella*, as well as to rarer ones like *Emmeline*
or *Juliana*. However, many exceptions can be found in families where this

---

[12]La Monte, "The Lords of Sidon."

[13]On the family of Tiberias, see Henry Pirie-Gordon, "The Reigning Princes of Galilee,"
English Historical Review 27 (1912), 445–61.

rule is very seldom followed, or indeed in which it is not followed at all. It seems to be more a custom than a fixed rule.

On the other hand the mother's name is very rarely given even when there are several daughters. An aunt's name, more often on the father's side, is usually chosen. For the younger daughters, an established rule does not seem to exist. Even though there is more originality in the choice of girls' names, there was nonetheless a respect for the traditions followed in the West both in the choice of names, usually common ones, and in the alternation of rules in naming, with the paternal grandmother having a predominant role. For girls and boys alike, the Latin East appears to be a place for the preservation of traditional names and the very rare, charming *Tourterelle*s or *Orgueilleuse*s remain the exception.

These few remarks, based upon the study of a rich and unique source, enable us to determine what the customs were that were followed by noble families of the Latin East when first names were chosen. The Latin East appears to have been a place for the preservation of traditional names that used name and naming rules common in the West without changing much. Much remains to be said about the role of feminine lineages, for example, as well as about the use of lineage names or of nicknames. But we hope we have begun to provide insight into the knowledge of the anthroponymical customs of these families.

Part V

Personal Names in the Later Middle Ages

Personal Naming among the Rural Populations in France at the End of the Middle Ages

Patrice Beck

Thanks to Céline Beck (Dijon), Hélène Durieux (Dijon), Richard Mowrer (UCLA), and George Beech (Western Michigan University).

The abundance and diversity of available documents surviving from the end of the Middle Ages facilitates the historical analysis of that period by scholars today. In addition to the essentially clerical and administrative data of earlier centuries, there is now evidence available from both lay society and from the private realm of the family. This new information gives better insight into the complexity of personal naming practices implied by the co-existence of names given at the time of christening, those given in the course of daily life, and those calling attention to administrative functions. It is also now possible to analyze family strategies interacting with socio-cultural constraints more effectively.

But it is also true that there are still numerous lacunae: studies have not been carried out in the same manner in all areas, the reconstitution of families is difficult, women rarely make an appearance in the data, and the distinction between town and country is not a clear one.[1] It is obvious that medievalists cannot do the same job as the modernists who work on serial

---

[1]François Menant, "L'anthroponymie du monde rural," in *L'anthroponymie. Document de l'histoire sociale des mondes méditerranéens médiévaux*, ed. Monique Bourin, Jean-Marie Martin, and François Menant, Collections de l'École française de Rome 226 (Rome, 1996), pp. 349–63.

sources[2] and the anthropologists who analyze living memories.[3]

However, the ways of naming people in rural France during the last two centuries of the Middle Ages can be described in rough outline so as to give an idea of the evolution of the anthroponymic system that took shape during the period between the eleventh and thirteenth centuries, and it is also possible to appreciate the distance yet to be covered before the system was formalized in the *code-civil* during the early nineteenth century.

Four main facts stand out clearly from the studies that have made contributions to the subject (see Additional Sources). The name composed of two elements did at last spread through the entire population; there was a continuing tendency to concentrate on choosing the names of the most important saints; clerical, administrative, and familial regulations on naming became more rigid; and a new conception of the name developed that was less dependent on etymological considerations in laying the grammatical basis for the proper name.

The Generalization of the Surname

At the end of the thirteenth century, 10 to 20 percent of laymen and 25 to 30 percent of clerics still had no officially recognized surnames. During the fourteenth and fifteenth centuries, the use of the surname for men increased and became standard everywhere, in Burgundy[4] as well as

---

[2]Jacques Dupaquier, "Prénoms, parrains, parenté—Recherche sur les familles du Vexin français de 1540 à 1900," *Mémoires de la Société historique et archéologique de Pontoise* 69 (1980), 55–87; and André Burguière, "Un nom pour soi. Le choix du nom de baptême en France sous l'Ancien Régime (XVIe–XVIIIe siècles)," *L'Homme* 20/4 (October–December 1980), 25–42.

[3]Françoise Zonabend, *La mémoire longue. Temps et histoires au village* (Paris, 1980).

[4]Patrice Beck, "Evolution des formes anthroponymiques en Bourgogne (900–1280)," in *Genèse médiévale de l'anthroponymie moderne* (= GMAM). *I. Études d'anthroponymie médiévale Ie et IIe rencontres, Azay-le-Ferron 1986 et 1987*, ed. Monique Bourin (1990), pp. 61–85.

in Lorraine,[5] in the Monts du Forez,[6] around Toulouse,[7] and in Provence.[8]

This evolution affected women as well, though more slowly, especially in the countryside. Seventy percent of women had a surname in Paris in 1300[9] as did 64 percent of women in the city of Blois in 1334,[10] but only 40 percent did in Burgundy at the beginning of the fifteenth century.[11] In any case their legal condition required that the names of both countrywomen and those of townswomen contain a reference to a man, whether their father, their husband, or their male children. When they happened to have a two-element name, the second name was often a man's surname changed to its feminine form.

Naming proceeded on the same basis in all provinces at the end of the fifteenth century. Surnames had been adapted and the sharp geographical and social disparities of two centuries earlier had been reduced or had even disappeared. North joined south, and the system initiated by the aristocracy was adopted by the non-nobility, by clerics, and by nearly all women.

---

[5]Patricia Dreyfus, "Étude du système anthroponymique de la ville de Metz au XIVe siècle d'après le cartulaire du Petit-Clairvaux de Metz" (Ph.D. diss., University of Paris I, 1996).

[6]Antoine Vallet, *Les noms de personnes du Forez et confins actuel département de la Loire) aux XIIe, XIIIe et XIVe siècles* (Paris, 1961).

[7]Pierre-Henri Billy, "Nommer à Toulouse aux XIe–XIVe siècles," in GMAM, *III. Enquêtes généalogiques et données prosopographiques*, ed. Monique Bourin and Pascal Chareille (1995), pp. 171–89.

[8]André Compan, *Étude d'anthroponymie provençale. Les noms de personne dans le comté de Nice aux XIIIe, XIVe et XVe siècles* (Lille, 1976).

[9]Caroline Bourlet, "L'anthroponymie à Paris à la fin du XIIIe siècle d'après les rôles de la taille du règne de Philippe le Bel," in GMAM, *II. Persistances du nom unique. 2, Désignation et anthroponymie des femmes. Méthodes statistiques pour l'anthroponymie*, ed. Monique Bourin and Pascal Chareille (1992), pp. 9–43.

[10]Jean-Paul Sauvage, "Formes anthroponymiques féminines à Blois à travers une liste d'habitants de 1334," in GMAM II.2, ed. Bourin and Chareille, pp. 45–66.

[11]Patrice Beck, "Anthroponymie et désignation des femmes en Bourgogne (Xe–XIVe siècles)," in GMAM II.2, ed. Bourin and Chareille, pp. 89–100.

Only the typological distribution of the second naming element retained a certain diversity by preserving, to a degree, regional and social distinctions. Those based on a Christian name, inherited from the *nomen paternum*, remained in the majority in Provence[12] but they trailed far behind the anthropotoponyms of rural Burgundy,[13] Normandy,[14] Paris,[15] and Metz.[16] In these northern areas the majority of surnames were taken from local place names, though certainly to varying degrees, according to the importance taken by names of professions (which affected the middleclass), and nicknames (which tended to be taken by the non-nobility).

It is clear that this evolution took place without the help of the law. The general practice, approved by legal authorities, was that people were free to choose their names. Public authorities began to intervene only in the fifteenth century in order to punish and prevent violations, or to authenticate voluntary name changing. The first surviving letter concerning name changing dates from 1402. The first general act enforcing the registration of individual identity is included within the Edict of Villers-Cotterêts in 1539, and this text simply confirmed the old clerical practice of maintaining parish registers.[17]

Choosing the First Name: The Role of the Church

The movement to concentrate choices on a very few Christian names, taken from the accepted repertoire of the Roman Catholic Church,

---

[12]Compan, *Étude d'anthroponymie provençale.*

[13]Beck, "Evolution des formes anthroponymiques."

[14]Marie Thérèse Morlet, *Étude d'anthroponymie picarde, les noms de personne en Haute Picardie aux XIIIe, XIVe et XVe siècles* (Amiens, 1967).

[15]Bourlet, "L'anthroponymie à Paris."

[16]Dreyfus, "Étude du système anthroponymique."

[17]*Le nom. Droit et histoire*, ed. Anne Lefebvre-Teillard (Paris, 1990).

had been initiated and developed before 1250. It has remained in force from that time forward, largely blurring, though not eliminating, the differences between men and women, geographical regions, and socio-economic disparities.

In fifteenth-century Burgundy, for example,[18] *Jean* accounted for up to 30 percent of the names chosen by laymen among the non-nobility, a little less frequently in towns, a little more frequently in the country. *Jean* was followed by *Pierre* and *Guillaume*, each comprising 15 percent. These three names accounted for 60 percent of the laymen registered in 1470. Among the clerics accounted for in this region in 1475, *Jean*, with 35 percent, and *Pierre*, with 15 percent, were first and second most chosen. The only difference was that *Guillaume*, with five percent of the total amount, was overtaken by *Philibert*, the saint of the famous Abbey of Tournus, a name borne by nearly 10 percent of the men.

With regard to the aristocracy, among the 1,693 knights and horse-men counted in 1414, together with 230 archers or crossbowmen, *Jean* was far ahead, followed by *Guillaume* and *Pierre*. Women were affected by the same tendency toward concentration though to a lesser degree, and for a certain time oracular names were an alternative to the rising popularity of feminized forms of the main Christian saints' names. In 1370, *Bonotte* was the leading name with 23 percent, but fell to less than two percent in 1460 and was not represented at all in 1488. Its place was taken by *Jeanne*, which in 1460 accounted for 22 percent of all women's names, as much as the combined feminine forms of *Pierre* (*Pierrette*) and *Guillaume* (*Guil-lemette*) together. In the fifteenth century, 44 percent of the female popu-lation took these three Christian names and only one name of feminine origin, *Isabelle*, was competitive with them.

For both women and men, this tendency was generalized in all the areas studied. The influence of the Church was of prime importance everywhere: the majority of those selecting names settled on John the

---

[18]Patrice Beck, "Noms de baptême et structures sociales à Nuits à la fin du Moyen Âge," *Bulletin Philologique et Historique* (1980), 253–66.

Baptist or John the Apostle, or Peter, the first Bishop of Rome, after which came the martyrs of the early Church and famous religious figures whose popularity varied according to region. Guillaume de Volpiano, noted as a great builder of churches in Northern France in the eleventh century, was one example. Another was Dominique, the founder of the preaching friars in the southwest in the thirteenth century. Prominent saints' names led to the decline of oracular Christian names[19] and local saints' cults had an influence only on Christian names of secondary importance, such as *Philibert* in Burgundy, *Claude* in Jura, or *Leonard* and *Martial* in Limousin.[20]

Only a few, rarely-used names differentiated aristocracy from the rest of society: they gave some of their children names like *Dalmacius, Manasses, Morellus,* or *Rollandus*. But the influence of princely dynasties was no longer what it had once been. If *Raymond* retained some of its importance in southern France in the fourteenth and fifteenth centuries,[21] the Valois names *Philippe* and *Charles* were far from equaling the popularity of the Capetian names *Robert, Hugues,* and *Eudes* in France and in Burgundy down to the thirteenth century.[22]

The clerical impact upon personal naming was undeniable: it was a sign of the success of a Church triumphant from this time on, fully organized and endowed with solid institutions for social supervision. In that way, it mastered, if not the choice of the name properly speaking, at least the mechanism of its imposition, thanks to the ceremony of baptism and the institution of godparents. Since the twelfth century, baptizing children

---

[19]Jacques Heers, *L'occident aux XIVe et XVe siècles. Aspects économiques et sociaux* (Paris, 1963), p. 344.

[20]Louis Perouas et al., *Léonard, Marie, Jean et les autres. Les prénoms en Limousin depuis un millénaire* (Paris, 1984).

[21]Jean-Louis Biget, "L'évolution des noms de baptême en Languedoc au Moyen Age (IXe–XIVe siècles)," in *Liturgie et musique,* Cahiers de Fanjeaux 17 (Toulouse, 1982), pp. 297–341; Compan, *Étude d'anthroponymie provençale.*

[22]Beck, "Evolution des formes anthroponymiques."

had been systematically carried out and the baptismal name merged with the name given at birth to become the personal name. Also, from the twelfth century, godfathers more and more frequently gave their names to their godchildren: in the Limousin, from 65 to 80 percent did so in the fourteenth century, and this happened over 90 percent of the time in the eighteenth century.[23] Besides, it is obvious that the Church was not satisfied with controlling the time and principles involved. It also made every effort it could to persuade, suggest, and determine the choice. *Jean* and *Pierre* were mentioned as examples within the christening formulas expounded by the synods.[24]

But it is obvious too that the Church intervened in a dogmatic way only at a very late date, after the Council of Trent.[25] This circumspection came obviously from a desire not to clash with long-standing family customs. These customs, stated in the Gospel of Luke in the chapter recounting the birth and circumcision of the Precursor, asserted that the choice of the first name was a family matter and a family heritage.

Between the demands of blood and matrimonial relationships, which were by nature discontinuous and private, and the dogmatic aspirations toward universality on the part of the Church, the contradictions were fundamental. But quite obviously institutional adaptability made possible a harmonious integration of these different and opposing desires and the establishment of regulatory procedures for personal naming.

The Full Name Passed Down, but not Unchangeable

In choosing names, how did people get around the problem of the increasing difficulty of identification of individuals resulting from an

---

[23]Perouas et al., *Léonard, Marie, Jean.*

[24]Paris, Bibliothèque Nationale. *Les Statuts synodaux français du XIIIe siècle. Précédés de l'historique de synode diocésain depuis ses origines*, 4 vols., trans. Odette Pontal (Paris, 1971).

[25]*Le nom*, ed. Lefebvre-Teillard.

ever-smaller stock of different names or the increasing frequency of different individuals bearing the same name? They did so through the use of surnames.

In the choice of the first name, how did people reconcile the customary demands of the family on the one hand and those of religious beliefs on the other? This was achieved through the possibility of changing the first name according to circumstances, through the intervention of the institution of godparents, and through the increasing use of hypocoristic forms and multiple, if not compound, names. When homonymy (i.e., two or more persons bearing the same name) became too oppressive, it was even possible to have more than one patronymic substitute.

The first practice, that of changing the first name of a living person in order to give him the name of a dead person, is abundantly documented in Tuscany.[26] It is also found within the French sphere to a lesser degree, probably in part because of the lack of adequate family documents. As a matter of fact, the medieval family books that survive for the Limousin do indeed provide examples.[27]

On the other hand, the second practice is in evidence everywhere. From at least the beginning of the thirteenth century (prior to that time there are too many lacunae in the sources to be certain), people developed conceptions of godparents that served the search for both worldly connections and heavenly patron saints.[28] It was, at first, quite possible to have several godfathers, though French synodal documents from the early thirteenth century proclaimed that more than three persons should not act as godfather to a child and to choose more would be demonically inspired. This proscription was often to demonstrate that the rule was widely

---

[26]Christiane Klapisch-Zuber, "Le nom refait: La transmission des prénoms à Florence (XIVe–XVIe siècles)," *L'Homme* 20/4 (October–December 1980), 77–104.

[27]Perouas et al., *Léonard, Marie, Jean.*

[28]Christiane Klapisch-Zuber, "Parrains et filleuls. Une approche comparée de la France, l'Angleterre et l'Italie médiévales," *Medieval Prosopography* 6/2 (Autumn 1985), 51–77.

infringed upon and the practice tolerated.[29] But nothing makes it possible to be certain about the role of these various prohibitions in the naming of godchildren: in literary texts as well as in parish registers, only one name was generally mentioned. It was the name of a close relative, of a man for a boy, a woman for a girl: this way, family links between generations and lineages were tightened, the stock of names in use within the family was respected and perpetuated, and the matrimonial "market" was carefully preserved with kinship prohibitions concerning only people closely related by blood. This endogamic model had been imposed on the majority of French families since the fourteenth century and almost all of them were still affected by it in the eighteenth century. At that time, the very language was impregnated with its strong presence: in Provence, *pairin* (godfather) and *mairina* (godmother) were words used to address elderly people and, in the area of Tarn, they designated grandfather and grandmother.[30]

However, the monopoly was not complete. Another pattern, partially exogamic, appeared on the southern fringe of the French territory. In the Gevaudan region in the fifteenth century, godfathers and godmothers transmitted their first names even though they were generally chosen outside the immediate family, but they were selected by the father from among a network of friends according to their names, at least for the eldest.[31] Even if no obvious link can be shown, this practice seems to point to the transition from a Mediterranean pattern from Tuscany that relied on the choice of a godfather outside the family who did not give his name.[32]

It is also in Tuscany that the vogue of multiple Christian names appeared from at least the fourteenth century. In addition to the customary

---

[29] *Les Statuts synodaux français*, trans. Pontal.

[30] Agnès Fine, "L'héritage du nom de baptême," *Annales ESC* 4 (1987), 853–77.

[31] Philippe Maurice, "L'état civil des notaires du Gévaudan à la fin du Moyen Âge: choix des parrains, choix des noms," in GMAM, *IV. Discours sur le nom: normes, usages, imaginaire (VIe–XVIe siècles)*, ed. Patrice Beck (1997), pp. 179–209.

[32] Klapisch-Zuber, "Parrains et filleuls."

name taken from within the family, a second name, preferably religious, was given, and for political reasons, sometimes even a third one.[33] But in France, the practice of giving multiple names is only documented from the sixteenth century onward, first of all in Perpignan.[34] Then in the seventeenth century this practice spread widely to be followed in the eighteenth century by compound first names made up most often of the most popular names such as *Jean-Pierre*.[35]

The spectacular spread of name diminutives in the fourteenth century is thought by Maurice Berthe[36] to be linked to an increasingly apprehensive and unstable popular mentality reacting to a time of crisis. In any case the availability of hypocoristic name forms increased the possibilities of choice even while respecting and strengthening the popularity of the most frequently-occurring names. This was so in the region of Lyon in the fourteenth century. There were as many *Guillermet*s as there were *Guillaume*, and four times more *Jacquet* and *Jacquemet* than *Jacques*.[37] In Burgundy, as well as in Lorraine, *Jean* was changed into some ten variant forms.[38]

Complex name forms that combined several surnames appeared as early as the eleventh century and thereafter increased steadily, to the point that one out of every four or five persons was affected by the end of the Middle Ages. In the case where different members of the same family bore

---

[33]Christiane Klapisch-Zuber, "Constitution et variations temporelles des stock des prénoms," in *Le prénom, mode et histoire, les entretiens Mahler 1980*, ed. Jacques Dupaquier, Alain Bideau, and Marie-Elisabeth Ducreux (Paris, 1984), pp. 37–47.

[34]Jean Guibeaud, "Études sur les noms de baptême à Perpignan (1516–1738)," *Bulletin Philologique et Historique* (1899), in Burguiere, "Un nom pour soi."

[35]Burguiere, "Un nom pour soi."

[36]Maurice Berthe, *Le comté de Bigorre. Un milieu rural au bas Moyen Age* (Paris, 1976).

[37]Marie-Thérèse Lorcin, *Les Campagnes de la région lyonnaise aux XIVe et XVe siècles* (Lyon, 1974).

[38]Beck, "Evolution des formes anthroponymiques"; Dreyfus, "Étude du système anthroponymique."

identical names, professions or generations were specified: Jehan Gribouleux *clerc* (clerk) and Jehan Gribouleux *boucher* (butcher), or Jehan Le
Goux *le jeune* (junior) and Jehan Le Goux *l'aîné* (senior). These third terms
seem to have been complementary additions rather than real surnames.
But in other cases they came from the family name stock and thus perpetuated an ancestor's name: the Burgundian Guille Guienot alias Jacquin
took his name from the late Jaquin Guienot, his father; Jehan Le Goux
alias Michiel had a grandfather called Michiel Le Goux. Obviously, these
second surnames were no longer just individual designations; moreover,
they tended to replace the first surname and to be passed on to the following generation, perpetuating the identification of branches issuing
from a single family.[39]

Thus the Middle Ages put into place virtually all of the modern
naming system; it made use of every possible naming practice except the
compound name, which was developed in the eighteenth century. But the
system still had to be formalized by legal codification. This was the work
of the Tridentine Church and of royal administration during the Renaissance, though some efforts at formalization can be noticed by the end of
the fifteenth century.[40]

The late Middle Ages also made its influence felt on another level
that might have been even more basic, and which was in any case fundamental: the level of semantics and grammar.

From the Common to the Proper Noun

Since the beginning of the thirteenth century and the more frequent
use of French as the language of documents, the laws of linguistics had
started their work of selecting and purifying personal names as well as
other words of the language. In addition to numerous and continuous

---

[39] Beck, "Noms de baptême."

[40] *Le nom*, ed. Lefebvre-Teillard.

orthographical modifications, some changes were regular and rather systematic. There is, for instance, the example of the amputation or the agglutination of the article or the preposition announcing the surname, as well as the final substitutions or transformations into a suffixation according to regional linguistic influences.[41] The forms that used articles or prepositions vanished. In Burgundy, they affected 63 percent of the names mentioned in 1337; 50 percent in 1375; 10 percent in 1470.[42]

These formal transformations point out a real semantic and functional evolution of the personal name. With a preposition or an article, the second term (the surname) simply added more information concerning the man or the woman so designated, whether a location, a profession, a physical or a moral characteristic, and the designation remained dependent on the linguistic rules of the common noun. When the anthroponym lost the article or the preposition, it was set free from laws that governed the common noun and became a proper name for which the earlier meaning was no longer essential. This was therefore soon forgotten and masked by phonetic and orthographical transformations.[43]

The analysis of these phenomena was already known in the Middle Ages, in part developed by Roger Bacon in the thirteenth century who wrote in his *Opus Majus*: "It is a property of the article to indicate the verity of the thing. Nevertheless, this does not appear in Latin, as there is no article. Yet, the fact can be established in French."[44]

Beyond any doubt the modern personal naming system was ready for formalization and legal definition by the end of the Middle Ages.

---

[41]Albert Dauzat, *Les noms de personnes. Origine et évolution* (Paris, 1928).

[42]Beck, "Noms de baptême."

[43]Mariane Mulon and Henri Polge, "Sur l'époque de la fixation des surnoms en noms de famille dans les différentes provinces françaises," *Onoma* 14 (1964), 58–72.

[44]Serge Lusignan, "Le français et le latin aux XIIIe–XIVe siècles: pratique des langues et pensée linguistique," *Annales ESC* 4 (July–August 1987), 955–67.

Additional Sources

Books and articles in books

Beck, Patrice. "Anthroponymie et désignation des clercs en Bourgogne (Xe–XIVe siècles)." In *Génèse médiévale de l'anthroponymie moderne. II. Persistances du nom unique. 1, Le cas de la Bretagne. L'anthroponymie des clercs*, edited by Monique Bourin and Pascal Chareille, 99–104. Tours, 1992.

———. "Anthroponymie et désignation des femmes en Bourgogne (Xe–XIVe siècles)." In *Génèse médiévale de l'anthroponymie moderne. II. Persistances du nom unique. 2, Désignation et anthroponymie des femmes. Méthodes statistiques pour l'anthroponymie*, edited by Monique Bourin and Pascal Chareille, 89–100. Tours, 1992.

———. "De la transmission du nom et du surnom en Bourgogne au Moyen-Age (X–XVème siècles)." In *Génèse médiévale de l'anthroponymie moderne. III. Enquêtes généalogiques et données prosopographiques*, edited by Monique Bourin and Pascal Chareille, 123–41. Tours, 1995.

———. "Discours littéraires sur la dénomination." In *Génèse médiévale de l'anthroponymie moderne. IV. Discours sur le nom: normes, usages, imaginaire (VIe–XVIe siècles)*, edited by Patrice Beck, 121–61. Tours, 1997.

Klapisch-Zuber, Christiane. "Quel Moyen Age pour le nom?" In *L'anthroponymie. Document de l'histoire sociale des mondes méditerranéens médiévaux*, edited by Monique Bourin, Jean-Marie Martin, and François Menant, 473–80. Rome, 1996.

Neiske, Franz. "La transcription des noms dans les actes du Moyen Age." In *Génèse médiévale de l'anthroponymie moderne. III. Enquêtes généalogiques et données prosopographiques*, edited by Monique Bourin and Pascal Chareille, 25–37. Tours, 1995.

Parisse, Michel. "Sur-noms en interligne." In *Génèse médiévale de l'anthroponymie moderne. III. Enquêtes généalogiques et données prosopographiques*, edited by Monique Bourin and Pascal Chareille, 7–24. Tours, 1995.

Vincenot, Henri. *La vie quotidienne des paysans bourguignons au temps de Lamartine*. Paris, 1976.

Articles and Essays

Beck, Patrice. "Genèse médiévale de l'anthroponymie moderne (Xe–XVe siècles), acquis et perspectives de la recherche." In *Des noms et des hommes. L'homme et ses désignations des sociétés antiques à l'identifiant chiffré*, Sources-Travaux historiques 45–46 (1996): 79–86.

Collomb, Alain. "Le nom gardé, la dénomination personnelle en Haute-Provence aux XVIIe et XVIIIe siècles." *L'Homme* 20/4 (October–December 1980): 43–61.

Maitre, Jacques. "Les fréquences des prénoms de baptême en France. Rite de dénomination et linguistique statistique." *L'année sociologique* 3 (1964): 31–74.

Unpublished

Richard, Nicolas. "Parrainer et nommer. Transmission des prénoms et stratégies de parrainage en Auxois aux XVIIe et XVIIIe siècles." Ph.D. diss., University of Paris I, 1984.

PERSONAL NAMING AND REPRESENTATIONS OF FEMININE IDENTITY IN FRANCONIA IN THE LATER MIDDLE AGES

Joseph Morsel[1]

Der Vorgang der Namensgebung setzt ihre Bedeutung voraus, verleiht aber auch Bedeutung. Anonym sein, namenlos, ein Alptraum. Die Macht, die du dir über sie nimmst, indem du ihre richtige Namen in die wirklichen verwandelst. (Christa Wolf, Kindheitsmuster, 1976)

The study of the means of designation and identification of people is a very difficult task for the medievalist as it raises the problem of a possible gap between socially experienced identity (the one we are concerned about as historians) and the identity appearing in written sources. An anthropological digression shows this more concretely. In the northern part of today's Brazil, there exists a double anthroponymic system, an official system that is found on identity papers, on the notarized authentication of signatures, on bills, bank documents, etc., which associates the Christian name and grandfathers' surnames. But in daily life, within the family, among friends, on the job, in politics or sports, or in short, everywhere reputation counts, no one is called by his "name," nor even by his Christian name, but by a nickname (*apelido*). This can be either a

---

[1]I would like to thank here my friend Jean Kempf (Chambéry), who provided the first English version of this paper, which remains the basic part of the present text. And I would like to dedicate this paper to Dorothy and Manny Greene (Manhasset, N.Y.), because it is directly linked to my meeting with them—and incidentally because they are in a certain way (although merely formally, of course) concerned with phenomena that I describe here, as Dorothy represents the "bridge" between Manny and me, and "Manny" is not an official but a socially lived form of identification.

diminutive (*Roró* for *Rosario*), or a totemic name (*Biscoito*, "biscuit," to refer to the person's sweetness), or a specially coined name without any other referent than the person (*Pelé, Chembre, Xuxá,* etc.). Most of the time people do not even know any other way of calling the person with whom they are dealing, and it is the *apelido* that is entered in personal address books. If the sole sources available were "official" ones, we would be theorizing about a controlled naming system that had no collective usage. Conversely, rejecting that naming system would lead us to ignore the use of kinship underlying the official identity of the persons under consideration, which is nevertheless a socially ratified way of identification.

This is why, when dealing with the results of anthroponymic studies done on textual sources, we must ask ourselves: what anthroponomy are we talking about? What sort of bias is introduced by literacy in general and more specifically by official writing practices? How can we connect the observed phenomena and the real construction of identity, if we assume that these phenomena are never simple and irreducible representations? Comparative studies have been conducted between varied textual sources and epigraphic inscriptions. These have obvious limitations due to a lack of correspondence between the categories of people involved (clerics vs. lay men, men vs. women, living vs. dead), the time gap (while the person was alive vs. after death), and the expected physical gap (texts that were meant to travel and were thus designed to self-contextualize their object, vs. inscriptions contextualized by their immediate environment).[2] Moreover, it may be remarked that these studies are limited to written documents.

---

[2]Monique Bourin, "Eine vergleichende Betrachtung der Personenbenennung in Urkunden und Inschriften am Beispiel des Languedoc," in *Personennamen und Identität. Namengebung und Namengebrauch als Anzeiger individueller Bestimmung und Gruppenbezogener Zuordnung,* ed. Reinhard Härtel (Graz, 1997), pp. 237–52; Hermann Falkner, "Zum Namengebrauch in administrativen Quellen Kärntens und Friauls," ibid, pp. 395–407; Heidrun Zettelbauer, "Der Namengebrauch in den Nekrologien und Urkunden Kärntens und Friauls von der Mitte des 12. bis zur Mitte des 13. Jahrhunderts," ibid., pp. 409–21.

This is why I suggest using an additional type of source that has a great many advantages: seals.[3] Seals are indeed used simultaneously with texts, and thus there is neither any significant difference between the categories of people mentioned in the sources and those who use seals, nor any temporal nor spatial gaps, as it were. Furthermore, seals are most interesting in that they combine the textual and iconic dimensions, which allows us to grasp the identity of the person using the seal in a non- or only partially textual way, especially given the fact that seals often carry coats-of-arms, the identity-conferring quality of which was theorized as early as the Middle Ages.[4] Lastly, since we are confronted with medieval names that can very easily change from text to text as the named person appears as a lord, a husband, a wife, a widow, a charter granter,[5] etc. (which raises the problem of the representivity of the forms preserved in sources that are always incomplete), seals give a stable and lasting representation of identity because they were not changed for every new use. By examining the seal and the text to which it is affixed, it is thus possible to find information going much beyond the anthroponyms written on it.

Seals, however, have certain drawbacks that have firstly to do with their appearing fairly late. This prevents us from going back before the twelfth century and even before the thirteenth century for the lower

---

[3]The seals used in this study have been located with the aid of the file for seals attached to charters (to the year 1401) preserved in public archives in Bavaria (including also Franconia and Swabia), which has been created in the State Archives in Munich. Moreover, Professor Stuart Jenks (Erlangen-Nurnberg) had graciously agreed to share with me the findings he made when preparing his article, "Frauensiegel in den Würzburger Urkunden des 14. Jahrhundert," *Zeitschrift für bayerische Landesgeschichte* 45 (1982), 541–53. I would like to thank him here for this help.

[4]Michel Pastoureau, "Du nom à l'armoirie. Héraldique et anthroponymie médiévales," in *Genèse médiévale de l'anthroponymie moderne* [= GMAM]. *IV. Discours sur le nom: normes, usages, imaginaire (VIe–XVIe siècles)*, ed. Patrice Beck (1997), p. 85.

[5]Bourin, "Eine vergleichende Betrachtung."

aristocracy, the group with which I am concerned here.[6] Also, because wax is fragile, many seals have disappeared or been damaged. Even if we admit that a great many seals have survived from medieval times (Pastoureau says three million have[7]) these limitations must be mentioned. Indeed, among the 336 instances of women using seals that I have thus far identified, I have only been able to use 236 seals, 31 of which cannot be read with full certainty. Only three date back to before 1301, five to 1326, and only 27 to 1351. The rest date back to 1351–1400. It is possible, nonetheless, to make some interesting observations. I will analyze here only seals used by women, especially in Franconia, upper Germany, as my study of the evolution of the aristocracy in this region at the end of the Middle Ages shows that the reorganization of aristocracy in the fourteenth and fifteenth centuries was based on a reconsideration of the function of women within the group that only then defined itself and was defined as "the nobility" (*der Adel*).[8]

---

[6]Jean-Luc Chassel, "L'usage du sceau au XIIe siècle," in *Le XIIe siècle. Mutations et renouveau en France dans la première moitié du XIIe siècle*, ed. Françoise Gasparri (Paris, 1994), pp. 61–102; Wolfhard Vahl, *Fränkische Rittersiegel. Eine sphragistisch-prosopographische Studie über den fränkischen Niederadel zwischen Regnitz, Pegnitz und Obermain im 13. und 14. Jahrhundert*, 2 vols. (Neustadt an der Aisch, 1997).

[7]"Du nom à l'armoirie," p. 89.

[8]Joseph Morsel, "Changements anthroponymiques et sociogenèse de la noblesse en Franconie à la fin du Moyen Âge," in GMAM, *III. Enquêtes généalogiques et données prosopographiques*, ed. Monique Bourin and Pascal Chareille (1995), pp. 102–10, and "Die Erfindung des Adels. Zur Soziogenese des Adels am Ende des Mittelalters – Das Beispiel Frankens," in *Nobilitas. Funktion und Repräsentation des Adels in Alteuropa*, ed. Otto Gerhard Oexle and Werner Paravicini (Göttingen, 1997), pp. 312–75. This last paper has been newly published in an English (and reduced) version as follows: "Inventing a Social Category: The Sociogenesis of the Nobility at the End of the Middle Ages," in *Ordering the Middle Ages. Perspectives on Intellectual and Practical Modes of Shaping Social Relations*, ed. Bernhard Jussen (Philadelphia, 2001), pp. 199–240.

Modes of Identification of Women in the Lower Aristocracy

As far as the naming of women is concerned in charters confirmed by women's seals, it may be observed that three-quarters of them deal with spouses, designated only by their Christian names and being characterized as the "wife of" such a man who himself is designated by his Christian name and his father's surname. There are also a few statistically non-significant women designated only by their Christian names and as "mother," "daughter," "daughter-in-law," or "sister" of one or several men; in particular, 10 percent of women are designated as "widow of." Thus, in almost 90 percent of cases, women do not even have a surname (not even their husband's) and are identified only by their relation to the male relative mentioned in the document, in general their husbands, living or dead. In the other cases, women either bear their husband's name (whether he is living or deceased) directly following their Christian name (two percent), or in most cases they bear their father's name, whether they were widows (five percent) or married women (three percent). There are also a few women who have a family name that cannot be ascribed with certainty to either father or husband. Chances are that they were in fact unmarried women bearing their father's name. According to the text of the charters, the married woman thus appears to have been clearly in her husband's shadow as far as identity is concerned,[9] and it was only after 1340–50, and especially 1360, that one began to see married women called (although rarely) by their father's name.

Seals show a different picture. The oldest five surviving ones (dating 1272, 1277, 1286, 1315, and 1316) are those used by widows. Indeed, the women represented by these seals no longer had a husband to act in their names, and significantly, the first three of these seals are in fact the

---

[9]This is not a specialized instance but a common situation in western Europe: see Monique Bourin, "Les difficultés d'une étude de la désignation des femmes," in GMAM, *II. Persistances du nom unique. 2, Désignation et anthroponymie des femmes. Méthodes statistiques pour l'anthroponymie*, ed. Monique Bourin and Pascal Chareille (1992), p. 2.

Figure 1. Seal used in 1286 by *Albradis*, widow of Albrecht von Scherenberg. StAW, WU 5426.

husband's seal used by the widow (which in two cases says "my seal": see Figure 1[10]). The first seal actually belonging to a woman from the lower aristocracy is one used in 1315 by *Hedwigis relicta quondam Hiltbrandi de Saunenshein* (Figure 2). This is a round seal displaying not a shield, but a bird on the field. Similarly, most women's seals from the upper aristocracy at the end of the thirteenth century show, rather than shields, a subject, perhaps religious, or an image of a woman, standing or riding, often with

---

[10]The widow *Albradis uxor quondam Alberti de Schernberk* declares in the text that *presentem paginam* [. . .] *tradidi sigili mei munimine roboratam*, but the seal (shield-shaped as it was common at the end of the thirteenth century) shows the canting arms of the Scherenbergs, and the caption reads: "✠ S[igilum]. ALBERTI. DE. SCHIRENBERCH." Staatsarchiv Würzberg (henceforth: StAW), WU 5426.

Figure 2. Seal used in 1315 by Hedwig, widow of Hildebrand von Seinsheim. StAW, WU 484.

a hunting bird.[11] The bird on this seal is probably just such a bird. The (damaged) caption reads: "*S. HEDEWIGIS.DE.SA (wnshei) N.*" On the seal, Hedwig bears her husband's surname, although the text refers to her only in relation to him as if she did not have a surname herself.

---

[11]Brigitte Bedos-Rezak, "Women, Seals and Power in Medieval France, 1150–1350," in *Women and Power in the Middle Ages*, ed. Mary Erler and Maryanne Kowaleski (Athens, Ga./London, 1988), pp. 61–82. Andrea Stieldorf, *Erste Zeugnisse für Besiegelung durch Frauen in rheinischen und westfälischen Territorien* (ms. Staatsexamsarbeit Bonn, 1992), and *Rheinische Frauensiegel. Zur rechtlichen und sozialen Stellung weltlicher Frauen im 13. und 14. Jahrhundert*, Rheinisches Archiv 142 (Cologne, 1999), p. 275.

Following these kinds of seals, we find a type not very common and not to be found after the 1360s, which shows the woman bearing both her husband's armories (sometimes in the inverse orientation) and name.[12] However, in the following decades, the majority of seals were of the three following types: first, there are seals to which I will refer as the "bridge woman" type. On these, the woman depicted carries in each hand an emblazoned shield, in general her husband's on her left and her father's on her right, and the caption almost always gives her her husband's name (I found only one exception).

On a seal used by a widow in 1353 who is referred to as "Kunne, lawful wife of the late Sir Heinrich von Sternberg, knight," the woman represented carries two shields from underneath (Figure 3: this is unusual, for women are generally represented carrying shields from the top). The shield on her left is that of the Sternbergs (bends), and the one on her right is that of the Seinsheims (pales). The caption reads "✠ *S'. KVNGVNDIS. DE. STERNBERG.*"

Another seal is affixed to the same charter of 1353 as the preceding one belonging to the daughter of Kunigunde von Sternberg, who accompanies her husband. They are referred to as "Dietrich Truchseß, knight, and Sophia, his lawful wife, daughter of the said late Heinrich von Sternberg." Thus, Sophia is identified only in relation to two men, her husband and her father. The woman represented on the seal (Figure 4) holds the Truchseß' coat-of-arms on her left (two fesses in checkered pattern), while the Sternbergs' coat-of-arms is now on the woman's right as it bears the armories of Sophia's father. The caption reads "*S'SVPHI DCI TRVS-SESIN*," which means that Sophia bears a feminized form (with the *-in* suffix) of her husband's name.

---

[12]For instance, there is the seal of Jutta von Steckelberg, wife of Ludwig von Thüngen, from 1358. It reproduces exactly her husband's seal (only smaller and with the heraldic crest in the other direction), which is itself appended to the same charter, with the legend: "Guta von Thüngen, spouse of Sir Ludwig" (*IVTE VON TVNGEN ERN LVEZEN WIRTIN*): Staatsarchiv Marburg, OIg, 1358/XII/10. A photograph of this seal is now in Joseph Morsel, *La noblesse contre le prince. L'espace social des Thüngen à la fin du Moyen Âge (Franconie, ca. 1250–1525)*, Beihefte der Francia 49 (Stuttgart, 2000), p. 687 (Fig. 6).

Figure 3. Seal used in 1353 by Kunigunde, widow of Knight Heinrich von Sternberg. StAW, WU 1033.

The principle of associating two shields, one of the woman's father and one of her husband, is also encountered in a type much less common in the lower aristocracy. This type puts two emblazoned shields side-by-side on the same field, a combination rather commonly found in the seals of women from the upper aristocracy.

The seal of Hedwig, affixed to a 1391 charter referring to her only as the "lawful wife" of Wolfram Schenk von Roßberg, displays the emblazoned shield of the Schenk von Roßberg (one medium fess), while on the opposite side displaying the emblazoned shield of the Guttenbergs (a flower with five petals). The caption is damaged but still partly legible, and reads "*SCHENCKEIN VON*" (Figure 5). This means that Hedwig was given her husband's surname (in a feminine form), as is the case on all seals displaying a "bridge woman."

Figure 4. Seal used in 1353 (same charter as in Figure 3) by Sophie, wife of Knight Dietrich Truchseß and daughter of the Kunigunde [von Sternberg] of Figure 3. StAW, WU 1033.

Much more frequently, and at nearly the same time (there was only a three-year difference in my corpus), seals appear on which women are given their husbands' surnames but on which the field bears only an emblazoned shield with the armories of their fathers. I will call this type "mixed."

An uncommon seal (Figure 6) as regards its caption is that belonging to "Kunne, lawful wife of Boppo" von Adelsheim, according to the 1347 text. The emblazoned shield (a donkey's head) is completely different from that of the Adelsheims (an ibex's horn) and could be that of the Bibereh-rens. The caption reads: "✠ *S. KVNEG' [undis]. VXOR' [is]. BOPP' [onis]. MILIT' [is]. DE. ADLOTSH' [heim]*."

Figure 6. Seal used in 1347 by Kunigunde, wife of Knight Boppo von Adelsheim. StAW, WU 886.

Figure 5. Seal used in 1391 by Hedwig, wife of Wolfram Schenk von Roßberg. StAW, WU 2541.

The most frequent type of caption is that found on the seal of Kunne, affixed to a 1351 charter, in which text she is referred to as "the lawful wife" of the knight Friedrich von Herbilstadt. The emblazoned shield is not that of the Herbilstadts (a vertical chevron) but is, rather, that of the Bibras (a rampant beaver). The caption reads: "✠ *S. KVNIGVNDIS. DE. HERVERLSTADT*" (Figure 7). Upon this seal, the woman is depicted as having a double identity, that of her birth through the emblazoned shield, and that of her marriage through the caption. This type of seal thus complements that of the "bridge woman," as the woman's two familial relationships (by birth and by marriage) are represented equally on it. However, it must be noted that the association of armories and birth is most strongly emphasized in this type of seal. As for her surname, it seems only to be used to indicate the family into which she has married. Incidentally, in the "bridge woman" type, the caption mentions only the husband's surname.

The connection between armories and birth is further emphasized in a last type of seal, of which I found only one rather early but isolated instance (1335) and which spread only after 1350 although it never really replaced the other two types. In this type the woman is referred to by both her father's armories and name, a type I will call "paternal": for instance, the seal of Elizabeth, affixed to a 1351 charter in which she is only referred to as the "lawful wife" of Squire Berthold von Bibra, shows an emblazoned shield with the armories of the Heßberg (party with 3 fesses and 3 flowers) and the caption: "✠ *S ELIZABET. DE. HESBRUC.*" (Figure 8).

While the text linked with this type of seal refers to the married woman in the traditional way, by putting her identity in the shadow of her husband's, the seal itself gives her a completely different family relationship. We are here confronted with two different notions of a woman's identity, one textual, and the other sigillographic or rather, to be more specific, heraldic, as if the armories (and thus the seal, as it bears only the armories and the birth name) were considered to be more "innate" than the name, which could change. In the fifteenth century it became more and more common in the announcements of seals at the end of the charters

Figure 7. Seal used in 1351 by Kunegunde, wife of Knight
Friedrich von Herbilstadt. StAW, WU 977.

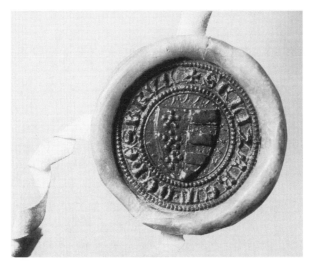

Figure 8. Seal used in 1351 by Elizabeth, wife of Berthold
von Bibra. StAW, WU 976.

Figure 9. Seal used in 1353 by Katherin, wife of Apel Küchenmeister. StAW, WU 6336.

to find the phrase *angeborenes Insiegel* or "inborn seal." Similarly, more and
more texts show that armories are considered to be the bearers of a per-
manent identity, free from possible changes of name.[13]

Lastly on this subject I will mention a rather curious type of seal on
which either a "bridge woman," or her father's emblazoned shield, or his
helmet with a heraldic crest appears, but in which the woman is referred
to only by her Christian name. On the seal used in 1353 by Katherin
(Figure 9) in a charter where she is referred to only as "the lawful wife" of

---

[13]Joseph Morsel, "Das Geschlecht als Repräsentation. Beobachtungen zur Verwandtschafts-
konstruktion im fränkischen Adel des späten Mittelalters," in *Die Repräsentation der
Gruppen. Texte-Bilder-Objekte*, ed. Otto Gerhard Oexle and Andrea von Hülsen-Esch
(Göttingen, 1998), pp. 259–325.

Squire Apel Küchenmeister, the woman holds the Küchenmeisters shield (with two fesses) on her right, and a chevronned shield on her left (which may be that of the Künsbergs). The caption reads: "*S. KA THERINE*" (the letters are widely spaced).

Comparison with Other Women

The study of the seals of women from the bourgeoisie (seventy items mostly from the cities of the diocese of Würzburg, all dating back to after 1360 except one) allows us some interesting comparisons. In texts, there is no significant difference in the way the women from the bourgeoisie and those from the aristocracy are referred to: "wife of" and "widow of" are found equally. The representation of identity in the seals, however, diverges significantly. The "bridge woman" type is almost never found (only one instance), the "mixed" and "paternal" types are found in equal proportions and gain ground but remain less frequent than the expression of the exclusive connection of the wife to her husband's family group (more and more often referred to as *Geschlecht*, that is, "lineage"). This is either represented by a seal bearing the names and armories of the woman's husband, who does not disappear (he is present in almost 20 percent of seals between 1376 and 1400, in contrast to the case with women from the aristocracy), or by a type of seal found only among city women, and associating husbands' names and a shield bearing the initial letter of the wives' Christian names (20 percent between 1376 and 1400).[14]

In both cases, and for about 40 percent of seals, there is no information about the women's birth *Geschlecht* but only about their belonging to their husbands' *Geschlecht*. This is a very different proportion from that to be found in the lower aristocracy. So, while the identity of women from

---

[14]StAW, WU 2010, 2203, 3214, 3561, 6137, 6203, 6265, 8045, 8141, 8155, 8175, 8179, 8189. See Jenks, "Frauensiegel," pp. 552–53. For instance, WU 2010 was sealed in 1366 with the seal of Kune, spouse of Heinrich Stuhs, from Würzburg. This seal presents the field with the letter "K" (in this case reversed), with the legend ✠ S. *KVNIGVNDIS. STVKSIN* (identical with WU 6137 from 1379).

the aristocracy as it appears on seals became progressively independent from their husbands' *Geschlecht*, the women of the bourgeoisie were still very much dependent upon it, despite the fact that seals appeared bearing the armories and/or names of their fathers.

We should not be surprised at finding parallels between the two categories of women. The rise of a barrier between the nobility and the non-nobility dates back to after 1400, and in the fourteenth century one could still see social and cultural connections between gentlemen and "patricians," beginning with family ties.[15] The differences encountered between women from the bourgeoisie and those from the aristocracy should not be seen outright as a sign of prior differences existing between the nobility and the non-nobility, but rather as the sign that this differentiation between nobility and non-nobility was implemented, among other things, through the construction of different representations of feminine identity. The difference between both social categories is not one of essence but one progressively constructed.

But the comparison with the seals of women from the highest, or "titled" aristocracy (at least earls or barons), is also most interesting. We have already developed some of these aspects, including the frequent presence of riding women or standing women with a falcon in hand, without armories, or the "bridge woman" type, or those with two shields side-by-side, which became even more frequent during the fifteenth century. Quite frequent also were the "party" or "*écartelé*" type, found extremely rarely among the lower aristocracy. The captions generally give the woman her husband's name, in fact his title, except when she is of a higher rank. But the development of a type including only the armories of a woman's father together with her father's or her husband's name (as in the lower aristocracy) is not to be found.

Thus, the identity at birth of the women from the upper aristocracy, although never neglected, is not represented as in the lower aristocracy, and is only marginally represented in the bourgeoisie, probably after the

---

[15]Morsel, "Die Erfindung," pp. 333–34.

manner of the aristocracy. Indeed, in the lower aristocracy the birth *Geschlecht* became an essential and indelible reference point, even after marriage. This would tie in with the fact that the notion of *Geschlecht* seems to occupy only a minor position in the upper aristocracy's kinship imagination, as opposed to the notion of *Stamm und Name* (race and name). So, while the *Geschlecht* seems to focus around the coats-of-arms, the *Stamm* would be more linked to the anthroponymic aspect (the *Name*).[16] The safeguarding of the interests of the name connected with precise heraldic signs in the lower aristocracy would correspond in the upper aristocracy with the preservation of the interests of the name, which acted there as a rallying cry until the eighteenth century.[17]

Perspectives

If we now try to sum up the information produced by the study of women's seals in the thirteenth and fourteenth centuries, the first thing to note is the difference between results based only on texts and those based on seals. The two modes of identification (naming in the text, including the announcement of the seal on the one hand; surname and coat-of-arms on the seal on the other hand) refer to two different representations of women's identity. Thus, one must be careful to separate the history of anthroponomy from that of identity, anthroponomy being only one form of representation of identity. In any anthroponymic study based on cartularies, especially those dating back to after the first use of seals, one must realize that the original documents undoubtedly bore different identity marks: women were referred to in different ways (in relation to a man or on their own), or were identified by different surnames

---

[16]Morsel, "Das Geschlecht," p. 266.

[17]In the lesser aristocracy, it was the *Geschlecht* that functioned as a slogan until the eighteenth century: see Christophe Duhamelle, "L'héritage collectif. Vocation, patrimoine et famille dans la noblesse rhénane aux XVIIe et XVIIIe siècles," *Actes de la Recherche en Sciences Sociales* 105 (1994), 37–45.

(husband's or father's) or coats-of-arms (husband's, husband's and father's, or only father's).

Furthermore, as far as the overall evolution is concerned, one must note the remarkable simultaneous and quantitatively balanced extension (until 1376) of both "intermediate" types ("bridge woman" and "mixed") in the lower aristocracy. Together they accounted for more than 60 percent of seals between 1326 and 1350 and for almost 60 percent between 1351 and 1376, each type accounting for half of those percentages.

After 1376, however, the "bridge woman" type plummeted as the type with the husband's name and coat-of-arms disappeared. The "mixed" type and the "paternal" type then accounted for about 80 percent of the seals between 1376 and 1400, the "mixed" type being slightly more common. In the fifteenth century, however, the "paternal" type spread widely, which is consistent with the expression "inborn seal" (*angeborenes Insiegel*). This shows us the reinforcement of the ideological connection between the woman and the family to which she was born, and there was no longer any perceptible difference between "paternal" seals and those of unmarried women. The evolution in frequency of the two types appears as inversely proportional to the degree of discursive integration of the woman into her husband's family.

In the second half of the fourteenth century, two opposing representations of feminine identity seem to have appeared on seals. On the one hand, there is matrimonial identity ("bridge woman" and "mixed" types), and on the other, birth identity ("paternal" type). Both, however, contrary to the text, reaffirm the birth identity, strongly linked to the coats-of-arms, against the name. This corresponds to the contemporary development of the discourse on the *Geschlecht* as the primary dimension of family connection. It was now presented as a descent that concerned men and women alike. Whatever happened, one remained a member of the *Geschlecht* to which one was born, a fact culminating with the adoption of "paternal" types of seals by married women, those seals being similar to those of unmarried women but also to those of the men from one's birth *Geschlecht*. The corollary is that the *Geschlecht* then became the social locus into which one married.[18] Underlying such evolutions in the representations of feminine identity, a change in the idea of matrimony was taking place. The woman who used to merge into her husband's *Geschlecht* now kept the indelible mark of her own *Geschlecht*. Marriage thus does not appear to have absorbed women anymore but rather to have positioned them between two *Geschlechter*.

The adoption of a "paternal" type (a parallel, as noted earlier, to the "mixed" type, but one that seems to question the representation of matrimony that was previously defining the identity of the married woman) can only be understood as an attempt at enhancing the *Geschlecht* as the real parental base, and as the decisive dimension when marriages were contracted. Marriage thus appears not so much as a union between two existing kins that merges them into one (which it actually does) as a union concluded between two *Geschlechter*. This point seems confirmed by the analysis of other forms of representations of feminine identity and their evolution.

From an anthroponymic point of view, we have been able to see that married women were occasionally referred to through their fathers' surnames in texts from the second half of the fourteenth century. This crystallized around 1400 into an anthroponymic system that then became widespread. The Christian name and husband's surname were followed by "born," followed by the surname of the woman's father. An example of this is *Anna von Reinstein geboren von Adelsheim*. Thus, where the seal tended to erase the matrimonial connection of the woman (the "paternal" type eventually becoming prevalent), the naming system tended to make her into the very symbol of the matrimonial alliance in which she was engaged, and an exclusive symbol at that, since the denomination of the married man was reduced from 1400 onwards to only his Christian name and surname while, in the 1370s, there were instances of men who added their mothers' surnames introduced by "called" (e.g., *Hans von Thüngen genannt von Eisenbach*, son of a Thüngen man and of an Eisenbach woman).

---

[18]Morsel, "Das Geschlecht," p. 277.

This diverging evolution of representations of masculine and feminine identities also appears on funeral monuments. It seems that, in the
second half of the fourteenth century (around 1360), the arms of fathers
and husbands appeared together on women's tombstones in Franconia,
such an association being very rare on men's tombstones between 1360
and 1400 (even with the father's arms and those of the wife, or with the
arms of the father and the mother) and disappearing later on, to be replaced only by the emblazoned and timbered shield (a form already most
frequent in the fourteenth century).[19]

Texts, seals, and arms engraved on tombstones are very different
modes of representation of identity, not only in semiotic terms but also in
terms of their social functions and their relationship to the individual.
Texts are associated with a specific moment in life, seals with a longer
period, as in the case of marriage, and tombstones are associated with an
eternal image. However, all these very different modes of representation
seem to converge. They place the woman in a position to represent the
matrimonial alliance, while they ground the man in what is most frequently called the *Geschlecht,* presented as a descent but which is in fact
only a successional group, the function of which is fundamentally to
transmit seigneurial power and title. The word *Geschlecht* should probably
be translated as "seigneurial line."

Thus, in the lower aristocracy, there was a two-fold discourse regarding kinship organization. On the one hand, the married woman was
positioned between two *Geschlechter,* that of her father and that of her
husband. On the other hand, and at the same time, this required necessarily and logically the conceiving of the *Geschlecht* as the basic social reality
of aristocratic kinship; this construction meant in turn that the married
woman had to get assigned a place separate and apart from the men inside

---

[19]Morsel, "Das Geschlecht," pp. 278–83, and "La noblesse dans la mort. Sociogenèse
funéraire du groupe nobiliaire en Franconie (XIVe–XVIe s.)," in *Autour des morts: Mémoire
et identité. Actes du Ve colloque international sur la sociabilité,* ed. Olivier Dumoulin and
Françoise Thelamon (Mont-Saint-Aignan, 2001), pp. 387–408.

the *Geschlecht*. Marriage contracts that appeared during the same period organized and represented the situation of the woman as intermediate through what constituted the favored instrument of social positioning in the Middle Ages, the circulation of symbolic goods. Indeed, the dowry was composed of specific goods different from those that circulated from fathers to sons (lands, castles, arms and horses, cash) or, when there was no male heir, more and more agnatically from one to another male member of the *Geschlecht*. Conversely, the dowry was composed only of rents, that circulated obviously from *Geschlecht* to *Geschlecht*.

Just as were the lands, castles, etc., so was the man conceived as *belonging* to the *Geschlecht* of his forefathers. The reduction that we observed in the composition of the "surnames" for men around 1400 must be seen not so much as a "reflection" of a change in kinship structures as the instrument of a change in the discourse on kinship as paradigmatic in the discourse on social belonging.

Indeed, the decade before 1400 and those just after 1400 were characterized by a deep restructuring both of the modes of organization of aristocracy and of the discourses on aristocracy against forces that seemed to question the traditional power of the lords, namely the territorial princes and the cities. It is in this context that the term *Adel* appeared in the late 1420s as a means of referring to the nobility as a group that was then explicitly opposed to the cities (*die Städte),* and to which the princes were clearly anchored.[20] The various representations given of the *Adel* make it a group structured matrimonially as a chain of *Geschlechter* connected by marriages.

Matrimony is thus not only a social act in which society's legitimate biological and social reproduction is based, but it becomes a discourse, a means of presenting the nobility as an integrated group. The role of matrimony in the structuring and integration of the *Adel* explains why the aristocratic exclusion (for instance, the right to capitulary prebends or to take part in tournaments) was based on a count of quarters and not of

---

[20]Morsel, "Die Erfindung," further "Inventing a Social Category."

degrees of noble lineage as in France. While the latter system was based on a notion of nobility in terms of seniority (hence the idea of "immemorial nobility"), the quarter system was based on an idea of nobility as a matrimonial network in which the depth of the matrimonial integration acted as discriminating factor.

As matrimony was defined as an act of constructing nobility by repositioning the woman between the two *Geschlechter* connected by matrimony, married women thus came discursively to be those in charge of the integration and reproduction of the *Adel,* while the reproduction of the *Geschlecht* was assigned to men. This function of the woman in the integration of the nobility is particularly obvious in the organization of the great tournaments in upper Germany in the fifteenth century.[21] While the tournament itself took place in public and formed the social drama of the *Adel* before the audience of princes and city folk, it was framed by two crucial moments, one opening it and the other closing it. Women played a decisive role in both moments because they acted as operators of selection: first the selection of the participants (*Helmteilung*), then the ball (which was a ritualized and euphemized form of "mating"), which cannot possibly be regarded as mere courtesy, as if courtesy had a meaning in itself.

One thus understands the impact of the changes in the seal representations of the lower aristocracy. These changes appear distinctive to the social group that was then in the process of structuring itself and providing itself with means of representation to confront the princes and the urban communities. The new representations of women in seals, though they are for the historian evidence of changes, should not be considered as a mere

---

[21]Joseph Morsel, "Le tournoi, mode d'éducation politique en Allemagne à la fin du Moyen Âge," in *Éducation, apprentissages, initiation au Moyen Âge* (Montpellier, 1993), pp. 310–31; Andreas Ranft, "Die Turniere der Vier Lande: genossenschaftlicher Hof und Selbstbehauptung des niederen Adels," *Zeitschrift für die Geschichte des Oberrheins* 142 (1994), 83–102; W. Henry Jackson, "The Tournament and Chivalry in German Tournament Books of the Sixteenth Century and in Literary Works of Emperor Maximilian I," in *The Ideals and Practice of Medieval Knighthood: Papers from the First and Second Strawberry Hill Conferences,* ed. Christopher Harper-Bill and Ruth Harvey (Woodbridge, 1986), pp. 49–73.

"reflection" of these changes, or as irreducible representations that could only give an inkling of something beyond social change. Far from it, the change in seals must be considered one of the instruments used by a social group whose organization and sociogenesis could only be made possible by the representation of new codes of identity.

Moreover, the evolution of these codes of identity participates not so much in a change in the *kinship structure* (which seems by no way to change in the Middle Ages[22]) as in the *discourse on being of kinship* as a means of structuration of a larger social group than the family or even the whole kinship. This evolution or even production of identity codes would thus only demonstrate and contribute to the integration of people into larger, and socially more important groupings due to the fact that parental belonging appears to have had only limited importance in medieval society, with regard to what can be observed in most pre-industrial societies.[23] In the present case, the matter would be the integration *of* and *in* the aristocratic group which was going to be defined in discourse and practically: "the nobility" (*der Adel*). It follows from this that Duby's *mutation lignagère* should perhaps be questioned again from this point of view. Was it a mutation of the structure of aristocratic kinship, or only of the discourse on aristocratic kinship, being itself a part of a larger social restructuring? Indeed, we have to note that the period of decisive anthroponymic change in Europe (from the eleventh to the twelfth centuries onwards) takes place in a society where kinship has no structuring function anymore, and it corresponds less to a change in family structure than to the constitution and

---

[22]Anita Guerreau-Jalabert, "Prohibitions canoniques et stratégies matrimoniales dans l'aristocratie médiévale de la France du Nord," in *Épouser au plus proche. Inceste, prohibitions et stratégies matrimoniales autour de la Méditerranée*, ed. Pierre Bonte (Paris, 1994), pp. 293–321; "Parenté," in *Dictionnaire raisonné de l'Occident médiéval*, ed. Jacques Le Goff and Jean Claude Schmitt (Paris, 1999), pp. 861–76.

[23]About the secondary importance, and thus the unsharpness of parental belonging, see Guerreau-Jalabert, "Prohibitions," pp. 298–95; "Le désignation des relations et des groupes de parenté en latin médiéval," *Archivum Latininatis Medii Aevi* 56–57 (1988), 93, 108; and Morsel, *La noblesse*, pp. 57, 59.

definition of social, space-rooted communities, from the villages to Christianity, so that the change of identity markers could be seen as a social process, homogenizing and defining the community in relation to "the others," while at the same time distinguishing and clarifying the place of each member in the community.[24] The evolution of anthroponomy and other identity codes is not to be considered as a mere secondary result of the whole social change but as a central contribution to it. Supposing anthroponomy had finally very little to do with kinship?

---

[24]This is how one could attempt to understand the christianization of baptismal names as it is observed everywhere in the West, despite the fact that the Church does not appear to have tried to exercise pressure or to impose any particular teachings or doctrine on the subject. This phenomenon seems to me a strict corollary with another major development: the genesis of Christianity as a territorial community (see Jean Rupp, *L'idée de Chrétienté dans la pensée pontificale des origines à Innocent III* [Paris, 1939], pp. 56–59), and the redefinition of Christian identity.

CONTRIBUTORS

PATRICE BECK
Department of History, University of Paris I, Sorbonne

GEORGE BEECH
Professor emeritus, History, Western Michigan University

MONIQUE BOURIN
Department of History, University of Paris I, Sorbonne

PASCAL CHAREILLE
Department of History, University of Tours

BENOÎT CURSENTE
Director of Research, CNRS, FRAMESPA, University of Toulouse le Mirail

ROBERT DURAND
Professor emeritus, University of Nantes

PATRICK GEARY
Center for Medieval and Renaissance Studies, University of California-Los Angeles

CARLOS LALIENA
Department of History, University of Zaragoza

RÉGINE LE JAN
Department of History, University of Paris I, Sorbonne

JEAN-MARIE MARTIN
Director of Research, CNRS, Centre d'histoire de civilisation byzantines, Paris

PASCUAL MARTÍNEZ SOPENA
Department of History, University of Vallodolid

FRANÇOIS MENANT
Professor, École Nationale Superieure, Paris

JOSEPH MORSEL
Department of History, University of Paris I, Sorbonne

MARIE-ADELAÏDE NIELEN VANDEVOORDE
Archives Nationales, Paris

LLUÍS TO FIGUERAS
Department of History, University of Gerona

BIBLIOGRAPHY

Atsma, Hartmut, and Jean Vezin, eds. *Chartae latinae antiquiores*. Dietikon-Zurich: Urs Graf-Verlag, 1981.

Aurell, Martin. *La noblesse en Occident (Ve–XVe siècle)*. Paris: A. Colin, 1996.

———. *Les noces du comte. Mariage et pouvoir en Catalogne (785–1213)*. Paris: Sorbonne, 1995.

Barceló Torres, María del Carmen. *Minorías islámicas en el País Valenciano. Historia y dialecto*. Valencia: University of Valencia, 1984.

Barley, Niegel F. "Perspectives on Anglo-Saxon Names." *Semiotica* 11 (1974), 1–31.

Barthélemy, Dominique. *La mutation de l'an mil a-t-elle eu lieu? Servage et chevalerie dans la France des Xe et XIe siècles*. Paris: Fayard, 1997.

———. *La société dans le comté de Vendôme: de l'an mil au XIVe siècle*. Paris: Fayard, 1993.

Bartlett, Robert. *The Making of Europe: Conquest, Colonization and Cultural Change, 950–1350*. London: Allen Lane, 1993.

Bean, Susan S. "Ethnology and the Study of Proper Names." *Anthropological Linguistics* 22 (1980), 305–16.

Beceiro Pita, Isabel, and Ricardo Córdoba. *Parentesco, poder y mentalidad. La Nobleza Castellana, siglos XII–XV*. Madrid: Consejo Superior de Investigaciones Cientificas, 1990.

Beck, Patrice. "Noms de baptême et structures sociales à Nuits à la fin du Moyen Âge." *Bulletin Philologique et Historique* (1980), 253–66.

Bedos-Rezak, Brigitte. "Women, Seals and Power in Medieval France, 1150–1350." In *Women and Power in the Middle Ages*, ed. Mary Erler and Maryanne Kowaleski, 61–82. Athens: University of Georgia Press, 1988.

Beech, George. "Les noms de personne poitevins du IXe au XIIe siècle." *Revue internationale d'onomastique* 26 (1974), 81–100.

Bennett, Michael. "Spiritual Kinship and the Baptismal Name in Traditional European Society." In *Principalities, Powers and Estates: Studies in Medieval and Modern Government and Society*, ed. Leighton-O. Frappell, 1–13. Adelaide: Adelaide University Union Press, 1979.

Berthe, Maurice. *Le comté de Bigorre. Un milieu rural au bas Moyen Âge.* Paris: SEVPEN-École des hautes études en sciences sociales, 1976.

Beyer, Heinrich, Leopold Eltester, and Adam Goerz, eds. *Urkundenbuch zur Geschichte der mittelrheinishen Territorien.* Koblenz: Hölscher, 1860.

Biget, Jean-Louis. "L'évolution des noms de baptême en Languedoc au Moyen Age (IXe–XIVe siècles)." In *Liturgie et musique,* 297–341. Cahiers de Fanjeaux 17. Toulouse: E. Privat, 1982.

Bisson, Thomas N. "The Problem of Feudal Monarchy: Aragon, Catalonia, France." *Speculum* 53 (1978), 460–78.

Bloch, Marc. "Noms de personne et histoire sociale." *Annales d'histoire économique et sociale* 4/13 (1932), 67–69.

Bois, Guy. *La mutation de l'an mil. Lournand, village mâconnais de l'Antiquité au féodalisme.* Paris: Fayard, 1989.

Bolòs i Masclans, Jordi, and Josep Moran i Ocerinjauregui. *Repertori d'Antropònims catalans.* Barcelona: Institut d'estudis catalans, 1994.

Bonnassie, Pierre. "Du Rhône à la Galice: genèse et modalités du régime féodal." In *Structures féodales et féodalisme dans l'Occident méditerranéen*, 17–55. Collection de l'École française de Rome 44. Rome: École française de Rome, 1980.

Bonnassie, Pierre, and Pierre Guichard. "Les communautés rurales en Catalogne et dans le Pays Valencien (IXe–milieu XIVe siècle)." In *Les communautés villageoises en Europe occidentale, du Moyen Âge aux temps modernes*, 79–115. Auch [France]: Comité départemental du tourisme du Gers, 1984.

Bosch Vilá, Jacinto. "Los documentos árabes del archivo catedral de Huesca." *Revista del Instituto de Estudios Islámicos en Madrid* 5 (1957), 1–48.

Boswell, John. *The Royal Treasure: Muslim Communities under the Crown of Aragon in the Fourteenth Century*. New Haven: Yale University Press, 1977.

Bouchard, Constance B. "Family Structure and Family Consciousness among the Aristocracy in the Ninth to Eleventh Centuries." *Francia* 14 (1986), 639–58.

Bourin, Monique, Jean-Marie Martin, and François Menant, eds. *L'anthroponymie. Document de l'histoire sociale des mondes méditerranéens médiévaux*. Collection de l'École française de Rome 226. Rome: École française de Rome, 1996.

Brattö, Olof. *Nuovi studi di antroponimia fiorentina. I nomi meno frequenti del Libro di Montaperti (An. MCCLX)*. Stockholm: Almqvist & Wiksell, 1955.

———. *Studi di antroponimia fiorentina. Il libro di Montaperti (an. MCCLX)*. Göteborg: Elander, 1953.

Brossaud, Matthieu. "Les exemples portugais de Grijó et d'Arouca (Xe–XIIIe siecles)." Unpublished Ph.D. diss., University of Nantes, 1990.

Brouard, Nicolas. *L'extinction des noms de famille en France: une approche*. Dossiers et Recherches 27. Paris, 1989.

Brückner, Albert, ed. *Regesta Alsatiae aevi Merovingi et Karolini (496–918)*. Strasbourg: P. H. Heitz, 1949.

Brunel-Lobrichon, Geneviève, and Claudie Duhamel-Amado. *Au temps des troubadours: XIIe–XIIIe siècles*. Paris: Hachette, 1997.

Burguière, André. "Un nom pour soi. Le choix du nom de baptême en France sous l'Ancien Régime (XVIe–XVIIIe siècles)." *L'Homme* 20/4 (Oct.– Dec. 1980), 25–42.

Carpentier, Elizabeth. "Les prénoms à Orvieto à la fin du XIIIe siècle." In *Villes, bonnes villes, cités et capitales: Études d'histoire urbaine (XIIe–XVIIIe siècle) offertes à Bernard Chevalier*, ed. Monique Bourin, 371–79. Tours: University of Tours, 1989.

Carrasco Pérez, Juan. "El Camino navarro a Compostela: los espacios urbanos (siglos XII–XV)." In *Las peregrinaciones a Santiago de Compostela y San Salvador de Oviedo en la Edad Media*, ed. Juan Ignacio Ruiz de la Peña, 103–07. Oviedo: Servicio Publicaciones, 1993.

Chassel, Jean-Luc. "L'usage du sceau au XIIe siècle." In *Le XIIe siècle. Mutations et renouveau en France dans la première moitié du XIIe siècle*, ed. Françoise Gasparri, 61–102. Paris: Le Léopard d'or, 1994.

Clark, Cecily. "English Personal Names ca. 650–1300: Some Prosopographical Bearings." *Medieval Prosopography* 8/1 (1987), 31–60.

———. *Words, Names and History. Selected Writings of Cecily Clark*. Ed. Peter Jackson. Cambridge: D. S. Brewer, 1995.

Claude, Dietrich. *Adel, Kirche und Königtum im Westgotenreich*. Sigmaringen: J. Thorbecke, 1971.

Coelho, Maria Helena da Cruz, ed. *O mosteiro de Arouca do século X ao século XIII*. Coimbra: University of Coimbra, 1977.

Collins, Roger. "Visigothic Law and Regional Custom in Disputes in Early Medieval Spain." In *The Settlement of Disputes in Early Medieval Europe*, ed.

Wendy Davies and Paul Fouracre, 85–104. Cambridge: Cambridge University Press, 1986.

Compan, André. *Étude d'anthroponymie provençale. Les noms de personne dans le comté de Nice aux XIIIe, XIVe et XVe siècles.* Lille: University of Lille III, 1976.

Coussemaker, Ignace de, ed. *Cartulaire de l'abbaye de Cysoing et de ses dépendances.* Lille: Imprimerie Saint Augustin, 1886.

Cuozzo, Errico. *Catalogus baronum. Commentario.* Fonti per la Storia d'Italia 101. Rome: Nella sede dell'Istituto. 1984.

Cursente, Benoît. *Des maisons et des hommes. La Gascogne médiévale (XIe–XVe siècle).* Toulouse: Presses universitaires du Mirail, 1998.

Dauzat, Albert. *Les noms de personnes. Origine et évolution.* Paris: Delagrave, 1928.

Del Treppo, Mario, and Alfonso Leone. *Amalfi medioevale.* Naples: Giannini, 1977.

Dreyfus, Patricia. "Étude du système anthroponymique de la ville de Metz au XIVe siècle d'après le cartulaire du Petit-Clairvaux de Metz." Unpublished Ph.D. diss., University of Paris I, 1996.

Duby, Georges. *Hommes et structures du Moyen Age.* Paris: Mouton, 1973.

Duhamel-Amado, Claudie. "La famille aristocratique languedocienne. Parenté, patrimoine dans les vicomtés de Béziers et Agde (900–1170)." Thesis, University of Paris IV, 1995.

———. *Genèse des lignages méridionaux.* Toulouse: CNRS-University of Toulouse-Le Mirail, 2001.

Duhamelle, Christophe. "L'héritage collectif. Vocation, patrimoine et famille dans la noblesse rhénane aux XVIIe et XVIIIe siècles." *Actes de la Recherche en Sciences Sociales* 105 (1994), 37–45.

Dupâquier, Jacques. "Prénoms, parrains, parenté. Recherche sur les familles du Vexin français de 1540 à 1900." *Mémoires de la Société historique et archéologique de Pontoise* 69 (1980), 55–87.

Dupâquier, Jacques, and Denis Kessler. "Nos patronymes vont-ils disparaître?" In *La Société française au XIXe siècle*, ed. Jacques Dupâquier and Denis Kessler, 461–88. Paris: Fayard, 1992.

Durán Gudiol, Antonio. *Colección diplomática de la Catedral de Huesca*. Vol. 1 of 2. Zaragoza: Escuela de Estudios Medievales, 1965.

Durand, Robert. *Les campagnes portugaises entre Douro et Tage aux XIIe et XIIIe siècles*. Paris: Centro Cultural Português, 1982.

———, ed. *Le cartulaire Baio-Ferrado du monastère de Grijó, XIe–XIIIe siècles*. Paris: Centro Cultural Português, 1971.

Eckhardt, Karl August. *Irdische Unsterblichkeit. Germanischer Glaube an die Wiederkörperung in der Sippe*. Weimar: H. Böhlaus, 1937.

Emery, Richard W. "A Further Note on Medieval Surnames." *Medievalia et Humanistica* 9 (1955), 104–06.

———. "The Use of the Surname in the Study of Medieval Economic History." *Medievalia et Humanistica* 7 (1952), 43–50.

Ewig, Eugen. "Die Namengebung bei den ältesten Frankenkönigen und im merowingischen Königshaus." *Francia* 19 (1991), 41.

Fine, Agnès. "L'héritage du nom de baptême." *Annales ESC* 42/4 (July–Aug. 1987), 853–77.

Fletcher, Richard A. *The Quest for El Cid*. London: Hutchinson, 1989.

Folena, Gianfranco. *Culture e lingue nel Veneto medievale*. Padua: Editoriale programma, 1990.

———. "Gli antichi nomi di persona e la storia civile di Venezia." *Atti e Memorie dell'Istituto Veneto di Scienze, Lettere ed Arti, Classe di Scienze Morali, Lettere ed Arti* 129 (1970–71), 445–84.

Fontaine, Jacques, and Christine Pellistrandi, eds. *L'Europe héritière de l'Espagne wisigothique*. Madrid: Casa de Velásquez, 1992.

Freedman, Paul H. *The Origins of Peasant Servitude in Medieval Catalonia*. Cambridge: Cambridge University Press, 1991.

Fried, Johannes. "Elite und Ideologie oder die Nachfolgeordnung Karls des Grossens vom Jahre 813." In *La royauté et les élites dans l'Europe carolingienne (du début du IXe aux environs de 920)*, ed. Régine Le Jan, 90–109. Lille: Centre d'Histoire de l'Europe du Nord-Ouest, 1998.

García Arenal, Mercedes. "Documentos Árabes de Tudela y Tarazona." *Al-Qantara* 3 (1982), 26–72.

García de Cortázar, José Ángel. "Antroponimia en Navarra y Rioja en los siglos X a XII." In *Estudios de Historia Medieval. Homenaje a Luis Suárez*, ed. Luis Suárez Fernández et al., 175–91. Valladolid: University of Valladolid, 1991.

———. "Les communautés villageoises du nord de la Péninsule ibérique au Moyen Âge." In *Les communautés villageoises en Europe occidentale, du Moyen Age aux temps modernes*, 55–77. Auch [France]: Comité départemental du tourisme du Gers, 1984.

García Gallo, Antonio. "Los Fueros de Toledo." *Anuario de Historia del Derecho Español* 45 (1975), 341–488.

Gautier-Dalché, Jean. *Historia urbana de León y Castilla en la Edad Media (siglos IX–XIII)*. Madrid: Siglo Veintiuno, 1979.

Geary, Patrick. *Living with the Dead in the Middle Ages*. Ithaca: Cornell University Press, 1994.

———. *La mémoire et l'oubli à la fin du premier millénaire*. Trans. Jean-Pierre Ricard. Paris: Aubier, 1996.

Genèse médiévale de l'anthroponymie moderne. Vol. 1: *Études d'anthroponymie médiévale Ie et IIe rencontres, Azay-le-Ferron 1986 et 1987.* Ed. Monique Bourin. Tours: University of Tours, 1990.

Genèse médiévale de l'anthroponymie moderne. Vol. 2: *Persistances du nom unique.* Part 1: *Le cas de la Bretagne. L'anthroponymie des clercs.* Part 2: *Désignation et anthroponymie des femmes. Méthodes statistiques pour l'anthroponymie.* Ed. Monique Bourin and Pascal Chareille. Tours: University of Tours, 1992.

Genèse médiévale de l'anthroponymie moderne. Vol. 3: *Enquêtes généalogiques et données prosopographiques.* Ed. Monique Bourin and Pascal Chareille. Tours: University of Tours, 1995.

Genèse médiévale de l'anthroponymie moderne. Vol. 4: *Discours sur le nom: normes, usages, imaginaire (VIe–XVIe siècles).* Ed. Patrice Beck. Tours: University of Tours, 1997.

Geuenich, Dieter. "Vorbemerkungen zu einer philologischen Untersuchung frühmittelalterlicher Personennamen." In *Alemannica, Landeskundliche Beiträge. Festschrift für Bruno Boesch zum 65. Geburtstag, zugleich Alemannisches Jahrbuch 1973/75*, 118–42. Bühl/Baden: Verlag Konkordia, 1976.

Geuenich, Dieter, Wolfgang Haubrichs, and Jörg Jarnut, eds. *Nomen et gens: Zur Historischen Aussagekraft frühmittelalterlicher Personennamen.* Berlin: W. de Gruyter, 1997.

Giménez Soler, Andrés. *Don Juan Manuel. Biografía y Estudio crítico.* Zaragoza: Tip. La Académica, 1932.

Glöckner, Karl, ed. *Codex Laureshamensis.* 3 vols. Darmstadt: Verlag des Historischen Vereins für Hessen, 1929.

Goetz, Hans-Werner. "Nomen Feminile. Namen und Namengebung der Frauen im frühen Mittelalter." *Francia* 23/1 (1996), 99–134.

———. "Nomen. Zur Bedeutung von Personennamen in der frühmittelalterlichen Gesellschaft." In *Name und Geschichte*, ed. W. Kremer (forthcoming).

————. "Zur Namengebung bäuerlichen Schichten im Frühmittelalter. Untersuchungen und Berechnungen anhand des Polyptichons von Saint-Germain-des-Prés." *Francia* 15 (1987), 852–77.

————. "Zur Namengebung in der alamanischen Grundbesitzerschicht der Karolingerzeit. Ein Beitrag zur Familienforschung." *Zeitschrift für die Geschichte des Oberrheins* 133 (1985), 1–41.

Gonçalves, Iria. "Antroponimia das terras alcobacenses nos fins da Idade Média." *Do Tempo e da História* 5 (1972), 159–200.

Goody, Jack. *The Development of the Family and Marriage in Europe.* Cambridge: Cambridge University Press, 1983.

Grohmann, Alberto. *L'imposizione diretta nei comuni dell'Italia centrale nel XIII secolo. La libra di Perugia del 1285.* Rome: École française de Rome, 1986.

Guerreau-Jalabert, Anita. "Le désignation des relations et des groupes de parenté en latin médiéval." *Archivum Latininatis Medii Aevi* 56–57 (1988).

————. "Prohibitions canoniques et stratégies matrimoniales dans l'aristocratie médiévale de la France du Nord." In *Épouser au plus proche. Inceste, prohibitions et stratégies matrimoniales autour de la Méditerranée,* ed. Pierre Bonte, 293–321. Paris: École des hautes études en sciences sociales, 1994.

Hanks, Patrick. *Dictionary of American Family Names.* New York: Oxford University Press (forthcoming).

Hanks, Patrick, and Flavia Hodges. *A Dictionary of First Names.* Oxford: Oxford University Press, 1990.

————. *A Dictionary of Surnames.* Oxford: Oxford University Press, 1988.

Härtel, Reinhard, ed. *Personennamen und Identität. Namengebung und Namengebrauch als Anzeiger individueller Bestimmung und Gruppenbezogener Zuordnung.* Graz: Akademische Druck-u. Verlagsanstalt, 1997.

Heers, Jacques. *L'occident aux XIVe et XVe siècles. Aspects économiques et sociaux.* Paris: Presses universitaires de France, 1963.

Herlihy, David. "Tuscan Names, 1200–1530." *Renaissance Quarterly* (1988), 561–82.

Herlihy, David, and Christiane Klapisch-Zuber. *Les Toscans et leurs familles: une étude du "catasto" florentin de 1427.* Paris: École des hautes études en sciences sociales, 1978.

Hey, David. *Family Names and Family History.* London. Hambledon and London, 2000.

Higounet, Charles. "Mouvements de population dans le Midi de la France du XIe au XVe siècle, d'après les noms de personne et de lieu." In *Paysages et villages neufs du Moyen Age,* ed. Charles Higounet, 417–37. Bordeaux: Fédération historique de Sud-Ouest, 1975.

Higounet, Charles, Arlette Higounet-Nadal, and Nicole de Peña, eds. *Grand Cartulaire de la Sauve Majeure.* Bordeaux: Fédération historique du Sud-Ouest, 1996.

Hlawitschka, Eduard. *Die Anfänge des Hauses Habsburg-Lothringen. Genealogische Untersuchungen zur Geschichte Lothringens und des Reiches im 9., 10. und 11. Jahrhundert.* Sarrebrück: Minerva-Verlag Thinnes & Nolte, 1969.

Hoenerbach, Wilhelm. *Spanische-Islamische Urkunden aus der Zeit der Nasriden und Moriscos.* Bonn: University of Bonn, 1965.

Holzfurtner, Ludwig. "Untersuchungen zur Namengebung im frühen Mittelalter nach der bayerischen Quellen des achten und neunten Jahrhunderts." *Zeitschrift für die bayerische Landesgeschichte* 45 (1982), 3–21.

Jackson, W. Henry. "The Tournament and Chivalry in German Tournament Books of the Sixteenth Century and in Literary Works of Emperor Maximilian I." In *The Ideals and Practice of Medieval Knighthood: Papers from the First and Second Strawberry Hill Conferences,* ed. Christopher Harper-Bill and Ruth Harvey, 49–73. Woodbridge: Boydell Press, 1986.

Jenks, Stuart. "Frauensiegel in den Würzburger Urkunden des 14. Jahrhundert." *Zeitschrift für bayerische Landesgeschichte* 45 (1982), 541–53.

Kaufmann, Henning. *Ergänzungsband zu Ernst Förstemann, altdeutsche Personennamen.* Munich: W. Fink, 1968.

Keats-Rohan, Katherine S. B. *Domesday Descendants: a prosopography of persons occurring in English documents 1066–1166, II. Pipe Rolls to Cartae Baronum.* Woodbridge: Boydell Press, 2002.

———. *Domesday People: A Prosopography of Persons Occurring in English Documents, 1066–1166, I. Domesday Book.* Woodbridge: Boydell Press, 1999.

———, ed. *Family Trees and the Roots of Politics. The Prosopography of Britain and France from the Tenth to the Twelfth Century.* Woodbridge: Boydell Press, 1997.

Kedar, Benjamin Z. "Noms de saints et mentalités populaires à Gênes au XIVe siècle." *Le Moyen Âge* 73 (1967), 431–46.

———. "Toponymic Surnames as Evidence of Origin: Some Medieval Views." *Viator* 4 (1973), 123–29.

Klapisch-Zuber, Christiane. "Constitution et variations temporelles des stock des prénoms." In *Le prénom, mode et histoire, les entretiens Mahler 1980,* ed. Jacques Dupâquier, Alain Bideau, and Marie-Elisabeth Ducreux, 37–47. Paris: École des hautes études en sciences sociales, 1984.

———. *La maison et le nom. Stratégies et rituels dans l'Italie de la Renaissance.* Paris: École des hautes études en sciences sociales, 1990.

———. "Le nom refait: La transmission des prénoms à Florence (XIVe–XVIe siècles)." *L'Homme* 20/4 (Oct.–Dec. 1980), 77–104.

———. "Parrains et filleuls. Une approche comparée de la France, l'Angleterre et l'Italie médiévales." *Medieval Prosopography* 6/2 (1985), 51–77.

————. *Women, Family, and Ritual in Renaissance Italy.* Trans. Lydia Cochrane. Chicago: University of Chicago Press, 1985.

Klewitz, Hans-Walter. "Namengebung und Sippenbewußtsein in den deutschen Königsfamilien des 10.–12. Jahrhunderts." *Archiv für Urkundenforschung* 18 (1944), 23–37.

La Monte, John L. "The Lords of Caesarea in the Period of the Crusades." *Speculum* 22 (1947), 145–61.

————. "The Lords of Sidon." *Byzantion* 17 (1944–45), 183–211.

La Monte, John L., and Norton Downs. "The Lords of Bethsan in the Kingdoms of Jerusalem and Cyprus." *Medievalia et Humanistica* 6 (1950), 57–75.

La Roncière, Charles-Marie de. "L'influence des Franciscains dans la campagne de Florence au XIVe siècle (1280–1360)." *Mélanges de l'École française de Rome. Moyen Age, Temps modernes* 87 (1975), 27–103.

————. "Orientations pastorales du clergé, fin XIIIe–XIVe siècle: le témoignage de l'onomastique toscane." *Comptes-rendus de l'Académie des Inscriptions et Belles-Lettres* (1983), 43–64.

————, ed. *Tra preghiera e rivolta. Le folle toscane nel XIV secolo.* Rome: Jouvence, 1993.

Labarta, Ana. "La aljama de los musulmanes de Calatorao nombra procurador (documento árabe de 1451)." *Al-Qantara* 9 (1988), 511–17.

————. *La onomástica de los moriscos valencianos.* Madrid: Consejo Superior de Investigaciones Cientíﬁcas, 1987.

————. "Reconocimiento de tutela a un mudéjar de Daroca (documento árabe de 1477)." *Aragón en la Edad Media* 5 (1983), 207–17.

Lacarra, José María. "A propos de la colonisation 'franca' en Navarra et en Aragón." *Annales du Midi* 65 (1953), 331–42.

———. "Introducción al estudio de los mudéjares aragoneses." In *Aragón en la Edad Media. Estudios de economía y sociedad*, 2:7–23. Zaragoza: University of Zaragoza, 1979.

Ladero Quesada, Miguel Angel. "Los mudéjares de Castilla en la Baja Edad Media." In *Los mudéjares de Castilla y otros estudios de historia medieval andaluza*, ed. Miguel Angel Ladero Quesada, 11–132. Granada: University of Granada, 1989.

Laliena Corbera, Carlos, ed. *Documentos Municipales de Huesca, 1100–1350*. Huesca: Ayuntamiento de Huesca, 1988.

Larrea, Juan José. *La Navarre du IVe au XIIe siècle. Peuplement et société*. Brussels: De Boeck University, 1998.

Lawson, Edwin D. *More Names and Naming: An Annotated Bibliography*. Westport, Conn.: Greenwood Press, 1995.

———. *Personal Names and Naming: An Annotated Bibliography*. Westport, Conn.: Greenwood Press, 1987.

Le Jan, Régine. "Entre maîtres et dépendants: Réflexions sur la famille paysanne en Lotharingie, aux IXe et Xe siècles." In *Campagnes médiévales. L'homme et son espace. Études offertes à Robert Fossier*, ed. Elisabeth Mornet, 280–83. Paris: Sorbonne, 1995.

———. "L'épouse du comte au IXe siècle. Évolution d'un modèle et idéologie du pouvoir." In *Femmes et pouvoirs des femmes dans le haut Moyen Age et à Byzance*, ed. Stephane Lebecq, Régine Le Jan, Alain Dierkens, and Jean-Marie Sansterre, 65–73. Lille: Centre de recherche sur l'histoire de l'Europe du Nord-Ouest, 1999.

———. *Famille et pouvoir dans le monde franc (VIIe–Xe siècle). Essai d'anthropologie sociale*. Paris: Sorbonne, 1995.

———. "Nommer/identifier ou la puissance du nom dans la société du haut Moyen Age." *Des noms et des Hommes. Sources Travaux Historiques* 45/46 (1996), 47–56.

Lefebvre-Teillard, Anne, ed. *Le nom. Droit et histoire*. Paris: Presses universitaires de France, 1990.

Lexikon des Mittelalters. 10 vols. Munich: Artemis Verlag, 1980–99.

Livro Preto da Sé de Coimbra, ed. Arquivo da Universidade de Coimbra. 3 vols. Coimbra: University of Coimbra, 1977–79.

Lopez, Robert S. "Concerning Surnames and Places of Origin." *Medievalia et Humanistica* 8 (1954), 6–16.

Lorcin, Marie-Thérèse. *Les Campagnes de la région lyonnaise aux XIVe et XVe siècles*. Lyon: University of Lyon, 1974.

Lusignan, Serge. "Le français et le latin aux XIIIe–XIVe siècles: pratique des langues et pensée linguistique." *Annales ESC* 42/4 (July–Aug. 1987), 955–67.

Lynch, Joseph H. *Godparents and Kinship in Early Medieval Europe*. Princeton: Princeton University Press, 1986.

Macho Ortega, Francisco. "Condición social de los mudéjares aragoneses (siglo XV)." In *Memorias de la Facultad de Filosofía y Letras de la Universidad de Zaragoza*, 1:137–368. Zaragoza: University of Zaragoza, 1923.

Marquès, Josep M. *Escriptures de Santa Maria de Vilabetran (968–1300)*. Figueres: Institut d'Estudis Empordanesos, 1995.

Martin, Jean-Marie. "Aristocraties et seigneuries en Italie méridionale aux XIe et XIIe siècles: essai de typologie." *Journal des Savants* (1999), 227–59.

———. *Italies normandes. XIe–XIIe siècles*. Paris: Hachette, 1994.

———. *La Pouille du VIe au XIIe siècle*. Collection de l'École française de Rome 179. Rome: École française de Rome, 1993.

———. "Pratiques successorales en Italie méridionale (Xe–XIIe siècle): Romains, Grecs et Lombards." In *La transmission du patrimoine: Byzance et l'aire méditerranéenne*, ed. Joëlle Beaucamp and Gilbert Dagron, 189–210. Paris: De Boccard, 1998.

Martínez Sopena, Pascual. "Logroño y las villas riojanas entre los siglos XII y XIV." In *Historia de la ciudad de Logroño*, ed. José Angel Sesma Muñoz, 2:279–322. Logroño: Ibercaja, 1995.

———. "Parentesco y poder en León durante el siglo XI. La 'Casata' de Alfonso Díaz." *Studia Historica. Historia Medieval* 5 (1987), 33–87.

———. "Repoblaciones interiores, villas nuevas de los siglos XII y XIII." In *Despoblación y colonización del Valle del Duero, siglos XII–XX*, ed. IV Congreso de Estudios Medievales, 163–87. Madrid: Fundación Sánchez-Albornoz, 1995.

———. *La Tierra de Campos Occidental. Poblamiento, poder y comunidad del siglo X al XIII*. Valladolid: Institución Cultural Simancas de la Diputación Provincial de Valladolid, 1985.

———, ed. *Antroponimia y sociedad. Sistemas de identificación hispano-cristianos en los siglos IX a XIII*. Valladolid: University of Valladolid, 1995.

Martínez Sopena, Pascual, and María José Carbajo Serrano. "Notas sobre la colonización de Tierra de Campos en el siglo X: Villobera." In *El pasado histórico de Castilla y León*. Vol. 1: *Edad media*, 113–25. Burgos: Junta de Castilla y León, 1983.

Mattoso, José. "La littérature généalogique et la culture de la noblesse au Portugal (XIIIe–XIVe siècles)." *Bulletin des Études Portugaises et Brésiliennes* 44–45 (1985), 73–92.

———, ed. *Livro de Linhagens do Conde D. Pedro*. Lisbon: Academia das Ciências, 1980.

McKinley, Richard A. *A History of British Surnames*. London: Longman, 1990.

Mélanges de l'École française de Rome. Moyen âge, temps modernes: L'espace italien. 106/2 (1994), 107/1 (1995), and 110/1 (1998).

Menéndez Pidal, Ramón. *La España del Cid.* 4th ed. Madrid: Espasa-Calpe, 1947.

Meyerson, Mark. *The Muslims of Valencia in the Age of Fernando and Isabel: Between Coexistence and Crusade.* Berkeley: University of California Press, 1991.

Mínguez, José María. "Ruptura social e implantación del feudalismo en el Noroeste peninsular (siglos VIII–X)." *Studia Historica. Historia Medieval* 3/2 (1985), 7–32.

Mitterauer, Michael. *Ahnen und Heilige. Namengebung in der europäischen Geschichte.* Munich: C. H. Beck, 1993.

————. "Zur Nachbenennung nach Lebenden und Toten in Fürstenhäusern des Frühmittelalters." In *Gesellschaftsgeschichte. Festschrift für Karl Bosl zum 80. Geburtstag,* 1:386–99. Munich: R. Oldenbourg, 1988.

Molenat, Jean Pierre. "Quartiers et communautés à Tolède (XIIe–XVe siècles)." *En la España Medieval* 12 (1989), 163–89.

Montanos Ferrín, Emma. *La familia en la Alta Edad Media española.* Pamplona: University of Navarra, 1980.

Moreu-Rey, Enric. "Consideracions sobre l'antroponímia dels segles X i XI." *Miscellània Antoni M. Badia i Margarit* 3, *Estudis de llengua i literatura catalanes* 11 (Barcelona, 1985), 5–44.

Morlet, Marie-Thérèse. *Étude d'anthroponymie picarde. Les noms de personne en Haute Picardie aux XIIIe, XIVe et XVe siècles.* Amiens: Musée de Picardie, 1967.

Morsel, Joseph. "Die Erfindung des Adels. Zur Soziogenese des Adels am Ende des Mittelalters—Das Beispiel Frankens." In *Nobilitas. Funktion und Repräsentation des Adels in Alteuropa,* ed. Otto Gerhard Oexle and Werner Paravicini, 312–75. Göttingen: Vandenhoeck & Ruprecht, 1997.

————. "Das Geschlecht als Repräsentation. Beobachtungen zur Verwandtschaftskonstruktion im fränkischen Adel des späten Mittelalters." In *Die*

Repräsentation der Gruppen. Texte-Bilder-Objekte, ed. Otto Gerhard Oexle and Andrea von Hülsen-Esch, 259–325. Göttingen: Vandenhoeck & Ruprecht, 1998.

———. "Inventing a Social Category: The Sociogenesis of the Nobility at the End of the Middle Ages." In *Ordering the Middle Ages: Perspectives on Intellectual and Practical Modes of Shaping Social Relations*, ed. Bernhard Jussen, 199–240. Philadelphia: University of Pennsylvania Press, 2001.

———. *La noblesse contre le prince. L'espace social des Thüngen à la fin du Moyen Âge (Franconie, ca. 1250–1525)*. Beihefte der Francia 49. Stuttgart: Thorbecke, 2000.

———. "La noblesse et la mort. Sociogenèse funéraire du groupe nobiliaire en Franconie (XIVe–XVIe s.)." In *Autour des morts: Mémoire et identité. Actes du Ve colloque international sur la sociabilité*, ed. Olivier Dumoulin and Françoise Thelamon, 387–408. Mont-Saint-Aignan: University of Rouen, 2001.

———. "Le tournoi, mode d'éducation politique en Allemagne à la fin du Moyen Âge." In *Éducation, apprentissages, initiation au Moyen Âge*, 310–31. Montpellier: Centre de recherche interdisciplinaire sur la société et l'imaginaire au Moyen Âge, 1993.

Mulon, Mariane, and Henri Polge. "Sur l'époque de la fixation des surnoms en noms de famille dans les différentes provinces françaises." *Onoma* 14 (1964), 58–72.

Nelson, Lynn H. "Personal Name Analysis of Limited Bases of Data: Examples of Applications to Medieval Aragonese History." *Historical Methods: A Journal of Quantitative and Interdisciplinary History* 24 (1991), 4–15.

Nielen, Marie-Adelaïde. "Un livre méconnu des Assises de Jérusalem: les Lignages d'Outremer." *Bibliothèque de l'École des Chartes* 153 (Jan.–June 1995), 103–30.

Nonn, U. "Eine fränkische Adelssippe um 600. Zur Familie des Bischofs Berthram von Le Mans." *Frühmittelalterliche Studien* 9 (1975), 188–201.

Pallares, María Carmen, and Ermelindo Portela. "Aristocracia y sistema de parentesco en la Galicia de los siglos centrales de la Edad Media. El grupo de los Traba." *Hispania* 185 (1993), 823–40.

———. "Elementos para el análisis de la aristocracia alto-medieval de Galicia: parentesco y patrimonio." *Studia Historica. Historia Medieval* 5 (1987), 17–32.

"Parenté." In *Dictionnaire raisonné de l'Occident médiéval*, ed. Jacques Le Goff and Jean-Claude Schmitt, 861–76. Paris: Fayard, 1999.

Pastor Díaz de Garayo, Ernesto. *Castilla en el tránsito de la Antigüedad al Feudalismo. Poblamiento, poder político y estructura social del Arlanza al Duero (siglos VIII–XI).* Valladolid: Junta de Castilla y León, 1996.

Paterson, Linda M. *The World of the Troubadours: Medieval Occitan Society, c. 1100–c. 1300.* Cambridge: Cambridge University Press, 1993.

Perouas, Louis, et al. *Léonard, Marie, Jean et les autres. Les prénoms en Limousin depuis un millénaire.* Paris: Éditions du Centre national de la recherche scientifique, 1984.

Piel, Joseph, and José Mattoso, eds. *Livros velhos de Linhagens.* Lisbon: Academia das Ciências, 1980.

Pirie-Gordon, Henry. "The Reigning Princes of Galilee." *English Historical Review* 27 (1912), 445–61.

Postles, David A. "Notions of the Family, Lordship and the Evolution of Naming Processes in Medieval English Rural Society: A Regional Example." *Continuity and Change* 10 (1995), 169–98.

———. "Personal Naming Patterns of Peasants and Burgesses in Late Medieval England." *Medieval Prosopography* 12/1 (1991), 29–56.

Ranft, Andreas. "Die Turniere der Vier Lande: genossenschaftlicher Hof und Selbstbehauptung des niederen Adels." *Zeitschrift für die Geschichte des Oberrheins* 142 (1994), 83–102.

Reaney, Percy H. *A Dictionary of British Surnames.* 2nd ed. Corrections and additions by Richard M. Wilson. London: Routledge & K. Paul, 1976.

Redmonds, George. *Surnames and Genealogy: A New Approach.* Boston: New England Historic Genealogical Society, 1997.

Revel, Jacques. *Jeux d'échelles. La micro-analyse à l'expérience.* Paris: Seuil, 1996.

Richard, Jean. "Guy d'Ibelin, O.P., évêque de Limassol, et l'inventaire de ses biens." *Bulletin de correspondance hellénique* 74 (1950), 98–133.

Robb, H. Amanda, and Andrew Chesler. *Encyclopedia of American Family Names.* New York: HarperCollins, 1995.

Rogers, Colin D. *The Surname Detective: Investigating Surname Distribution in England, 1086–Present Day.* New York: St. Martin's Press, 1995.

Röhricht, Reinhold. *Additamentum.* Innsbruck: Libraria Academica Wagneriana, 1904.

———. *Regesta regni Hierosolymitani, 1097–1291.* Innsbruck: Libraria Academica Wagneriana, 1893.

Rüdt de Collenberg, Wipertus-Hugo. "Les Ibelins aux XIIIe–XIVe siècles." *Epeteris* 9 (1977–79), 117–265.

———. "Les premiers Ibelins." *Le Moyen Âge* (1965), 433–74.

———. "Les Raynouard, seigneurs de Néfin et de Maraclé en terre sainte et leur parenté en Languedoc." *Cahiers de civilisation médiévale* 7/3 (1964), 289–311.

———. *The Rupenides, Hethumides and Lusignans. The Structure of the Armeno-Cilician Dynasties.* Paris: Klincksieck, 1963.

Rupp, Jean. *L'idée de Chrétienté dans la pensée pontificale des origines à Innocent III.* Paris: Les Presses modernes, 1939.

Salazar Acha, Jaime de. "Los descendientes del conde Ero Fernández, fundador del monasterio de Santa María de Ferreira de Pallares." In *Galicia en la Edad Media*, 67–86. Madrid: Sociedad Española de Estudios Medievales, 1990.

Salvatori, Enrica. *La popolazione pisana nel Duecento (dal patto di alleanza di Pisa con Siena, Pistoia e Poggibonsi del 1228)*. Pisa: GISEM ETS, 1994.

Schmid, Karl. "Personenforschung und Namenforschung am Beispiel der Klostergemeinschaft von Fulda." *Frühmittelalterliche Studien* 5 (1971), 235–67.

———. "Zur Problematik von Familie, Sippe und Geschlecht, Haus und Dynastie, beim mittelalterlichen Adel. Vorfragen zum Thema 'Adel und Herrschaft im Mittelalter'." *Zeitschrift für die Geschichte des Oberrheins* 105 (1957), 1–62.

Schützeichel, Rudolf. "Zur Namenforschung." *Beiträge zur Namenforschung* 21 (1986), 1–13.

Siebs, Benno Eide. *Die Personennamen der Germanen*. Wiesbaden: M. Sändig, 1970.

Smith, Colin. "A Conjecture about the Authorship of the *Historia Roderici*." *Journal of Hispanic Research* 2/8 (1994), 175–81.

Smith, Elsdon C. *American Surnames*. Philadelphia: Chilton Book Co, 1969.

———. *Personal Names: A Bibliography*. New York: New York Public Library, 1952.

Les Statuts synodaux français du XIIIe siècle. Vol. 1: *Les statuts de Paris et le synodal de l'ouest: XIIIe siècle*. Publ. and trans. Odette Pontal. Collection de documents inédits sur l'histoire de France 9. Paris: Bibliothèque nationale, 1971.

Les Statuts synodaux français du XIIIe siècle. Vol. 2: *Les statuts de 1230 à 1260*. Publ. and trans. Odette Pontal. Collection de documents inédits sur l'histoire de France 15. Paris: Bibliothèque nationale, 1983.

Les Statuts synodaux français du XIIIe siècle. Vol. 3: *Les statuts synodaux angevins de la seconde moitié du XIIIe siècle. Précédés d'une étude sur la législation synodale angevine.* Publ. and trans. Joseph Avril. Collection de documents inédits sur l'histoire de France 19. Paris: Éd. du comité des travaux historiques et scientifiques, 1988.

Les Statuts synodaux français du XIIIe siècle. Vol. 4: *Les statuts synodaux de l'ancienne province de Reims, Cambrai, Arras, Noyon, Soisson et Tournai.* Publ. Joseph Avril. Collection de documents inédits sur l'histoire de France 23. Paris: Éd. du comité des travaux historiques et scientifiques, 1995.

Les Statuts synodaux français du XIIIe siècle. Vol. 5: *Les statuts synodaux des anciennes provinces de Bordeaux, Auch, Sens et Rouen: fin XIIIe siècle.* Introd. and Publ. Joseph Avril. Collection de documents inédits sur l'histoire de France 28. Paris: Éd. du comité des travaux historiques et scientifiques, 2001.

Stieldorf, Andrea. *Rheinische Frauensiegel. Zur rechtlichen und sozialen Stellung weltlicher Frauen im 13. und 14. Jahrhundert.* Rheinisches Archiv 142. Cologne: Böhlau, 1999.

Störmer, Wilhelm. *Früher Adel. Studien zur politischen Führungsschicht im fränkisch-deutschen Reich vom 8. bis 11. Jahrhundert.* Monographien zur Geschichte des Mittelalters 6. 2 vols. Stuttgart: A. Hiersemann, 1973.

Strayer, Joseph Reese, ed. *Dictionary of the Middle Ages.* New York: C. Scribner, 1982–.

Sublet, Jacqueline. *Le voile du nom. Essai sur le nom propre arabe.* Paris: Presses universitaires de France, 1991.

To Figueras, Lluís. *Família i hereu a la Catalunya nord-oriental (segles X–XII).* Barcelona: Abadia de Montserrat, 1997.

Toubert, Pierre. "L'institution du mariage chrétien, de l'Antiquité tardive à l'an mil." *Morfologie sociali e culturali in Europa fra tarda antichità e alto medioevo* 45 (1998), 503–53.

———. "La théorie du mariage chez les moralistes carolingiens." *Il Matrimonio nella società altomedieval* 24 (1977), 233–82.

Ubieto Arteta, Antonio. "Sobre demografia aragonesa del siglo XII." In *Quince temas medievales publicados por el profesor Don Antonio Ubieto*, ed. Antonio Ubieto Arteta, 219–39. Zaragoza: University of Zaragoza, 1991.

———, ed. *Crónicas anónimas de Sahagún*. Zaragoza: University of Zaragoza, 1987.

Vahl, Wolfhard. *Fränkische Rittersiegel. Eine sphragistisch-prosopographische Studie über den fränkischen Niederadel zwischen Regnitz, Pegnitz und Obermain im 13. und 14. Jahrhundert*. 2 vols. Neustadt an der Aisch: Degener, 1997.

Vallet, Antoine. *Les noms de personnes du Forez et confins (actuel département de la Loire) aux XIIe, XIIIe et XIVe siècles*. Paris: Société d'édition "Les Belles lettres," 1961.

Venturini, Alain. "Les noms de baptême de Nice et du pays niçois, XIIIe–XVe siècles." *Mémoires de l'Académie du Vaucluse* 6 (1985), 179–97.

Viguera Molins, María Jesús. "Dos nuevos documentos árabes de Aragón (Jarque y Morés, 1492)." *Aragón en la Edad Media* 4 (1981), 231–65.

Weidemann, Margarete. *Das Testament des Bischofs Berthramn von Le Mans vom 27. März 616. Untersuchungen zur Besitz und Geschichte einer fränkischen Familie im 6. und 7. Jahrhundert*. Mainz: Verlag des Römisch-Germanischen Zentralmuseums, 1986.

Werner, Karl-Ferdinand. "Liens de parenté et noms de personne. Un problème historique et méthodologique." In *Famille et parenté dans l'Occident médiéval*, ed. Georges Duby and Jacques Le Goff, 13–18. Collection de l'École française de Rome 30. Rome: L'École française de Rome, 1977.

Wilson, Stephen. *The Means of Naming: A Social and Cultural History of Personal Naming in Western Europe*. London: UCL Press, 1998.

Withycombe, Elizabeth G. *The Oxford Dictionary of English Christian Names*. 3rd ed. Oxford: Clarendon, 1977.

Woolf, Henry Bosley. *The Old Germanic Principles of Name-Giving*. Baltimore: The Johns Hopkins Press, 1939.

Zimmermann, Michel. "Aux origines de la Catalogne. Géographie politique et affirmation nationale." *Le Moyen Âge* 89 (1983), 5–40.

———. "Les débuts de la révolution anthroponymique en Catalogne (Xe–XIIe siècles)." In *Cadres de vie et société dans le Midi médiéval*, ed. Charles Higounet, Pierre Bonnassie, and Jean-Bernard Marquette, 289–308. Annales du Midi 102. Toulouse: E. Privat, 1990.

Zonabend, Françoise. *La mémoire longue. Temps et histoires au village*. Paris: Presses universitaires de France, 1980.